ENTREPRENEUR
JOURNEYS

ISBN: 1-4392-3451-5
ISBN-13: 9781439234518

Visit www.booksurge.com to order additional copies.

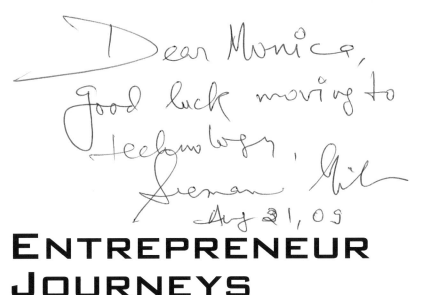

Dear Monica,
Good luck moving to
Technology,
Sramana [signature]
Aug 21, 09

ENTREPRENEUR JOURNEYS

VOLUME TWO

BOOTSTRAPPING: WEAPON OF MASS RECONSTRUCTION

SRAMANA MITRA

Sramana@alum.mit.edu
sramana@comcast.net

To my mother,
and the virtue of frugality.

Where the mind is without fear and the head is held high
Where knowledge is free
Where the world has not been broken up into fragments
By narrow domestic walls
Where words come out from the depths of truth
Where tireless striving stretches its arms toward perfection
Where the clear stream of reason has not lost its way
Into the dreary desert sand of dead habit
Where the mind is led forward by thee
Into ever-widening thought and action
Into that heaven of freedom, my Father, let our minds awake.

—**Rabindranath Tagore**

CONTENTS

i.	**Prologue**	xi
ii.	**Doing More with Less**	xiii
	a. The Real VCs Of Silicon Valley	1
	b. Fund Envy	5
	c. Bootstrapping, Montana Style	9
	Greg Gianforte, RightNow	13
iii.	**Getting Started with Little or No Capital**	29
	a. Passion and Leverage	31
	Cree Lawson, Travel Ad Network	35
	Beatrice Tarka, Mobissimo	49
	b. Barack Obama's Finance Lesson	59
	Om Malik, GigaOM	63
	Rafat Ali, paidContent	77
	J. R. Johnson, VirtualTourist	95
	Guillaume Cohen, Veodia	107
	Wayne Krause, Hydro Green Energy	121
	c. Weapon of Mass Reconstruction	133
	Scott Wainner, SysOpt and ResellerRatings	137
	Ramu Yalamanchi, hi5	149
iv.	**Validating The Market – On The Cheap**	163
	a. Carts Ahead Of Horses	165

		Murli Thirumale, Ocarina	167
		Manoj Saxena, Webify	181
v.	**Resurrecting The Dead**		**197**
	a.	Silicon Lazarus	199
		Lars Dalgaard, SuccessFactors	203
vi.	**Epilogue**		**229**

PROLOGUE

Much of this book was written in 2008, as Barack Obama ascended to the White House and Wall Street descended to the poor house. While Obama called for *hope* on billets in our shop windows and front lawns, on seemingly every bumper of every car on Bay Area roads – our financial market simply collapsed.

"What next?" was the question at the top of my mind. And as a result, readers will find this volume laced with political nuance, as well as a genuine attempt to understand what might deliver America, and the world at large, from its dire present day.

So, what next? Where to from here? From my perspective it is clear that small business must be a top policy priority. There are approximately five million small businesses in the United States with fewer than 20 employees. Another 20 million mom-and-pops endeavor day in and day out without employees. Let us hope that in the coming decade those numbers will double, then triple and quadruple. For here is the most powerful engine of economic growth and sustenance. Here is our way back.

If the next Google is to emerge and bring with it thousands of new jobs, it must first start over some kitchen table where not only hope, but opportunity is readily available. Where entrepreneurs not only start businesses at a higher rate, but also survive and thrive at a higher rate.

To achieve this we must answer several questions: Why don't more businesses get off the ground? And, once up, why do so many fail?

Through much discussion, writing, and brainstorming on each topic, I arrived at a core thesis: *Not just entrepreneurship, but bootstrapped entrepreneurship is the true weapon of mass reconstruction.*

Businesses often fail to take flight because they cannot raise funding. Well, start with the assumption that funding will not be available until the business is substantially further along, if ever, and that bottleneck is removed.

Additionally, most businesses should not look to raise money. As true small businesses – in the eyes of venture capitalists, even a $5 or $25 million business is considered a small business – they do not really fit the framework of professional venture capital. That does not, however, mean these businesses are not worth building. In fact, a $12-million-a-year company fully owned by the entrepreneur is a wonderful situation. Full control. Loads of cash. And true independence. Heck, even a $300,000-a-year business has many of those same attributes, and is more than worthwhile.

Now, why do so many small businesses fail? Undoubtedly there are many complex reasons, but a primary one is that they run out of cash. They use whatever resources they have imprudently, and end up destitute. The offices empty through rounds of layoffs. Boxes are packed, projects shelved. A final liquidation, and the unerring quiet of failure.

This though is not the inevitable end. In this volume, we explore a dozen stories of entrepreneurs who have mastered the art of doing more with less, creating a great many options in the process. And making clear for the world over that prosperity and independence are not mutually exclusive. That in fact they go best together.

DOING MORE WITH LESS

THE REAL VCs OF SILICON VALLEY

To understand the financing ecosystem in which startups play, it is important to first address some misconceptions. Chief among them is that VCs partake in early-stage investments.

While it is true that venture capitalists originally focused on early-stage, high-risk investment, today they have amassed huge war chests, raising funds set to eclipse one billion dollars. Even so, the number of people in most venture partnerships has remained relatively modest. You don't have to do much math to realize that such firms are forced to make bigger and bigger investments to generate adequate returns for their limited partners. Therein lies the problem for first-time entrepreneurs.

Of course, the bar has always been high for those trying to start out. Alex Osadzinski, a former general partner at Trinity Ventures, notes that most VCs are reluctant to fund a first-time CEO who hasn't held a key position in a previous startup. "If this is your first CEO job, and the first time in a startup, you're putting a steep learning curve in your way," warns Osadzinski. His advice: become the technical founder or vice president of marketing in someone else's company.

Very well, but that's a bucket of cold water for any entrepreneur with a burning passion. Besides, history is full of counterexamples – look at Steve Jobs or Bill Gates. Larry Page and Sergey Brin were young PhD students at Stanford University – their lack of experience couldn't stop Google from taking root. Similarly, Mark Zuckerberg delivered the Facebook phenomenon as if out of a hat.

The truth is, startup-land is littered with mavericks, iconoclasts, dropouts and misfits.

"It definitely makes it easier to raise money if you're a serial entrepreneur," concurs Venky Harinarayan, chief executive of search engine startup Kosmix. "That said, the prevailing VC wisdom is that serial entrepreneurs can get you great returns, but the franchise companies are created by first-timers." Those would be Microsoft, Google, Apple, Facebook, and dozens of others.

So how did these legendary entrepreneurs navigate the maze?

Lacking a better alternative, first-time entrepreneurs often turn to friends and family. Bill Gates funded Microsoft with family money, and the blessing of his parents. It's a dangerous path, though. Startups are prone to tough times, and these relationships can quickly strain. After all, prevailing wisdom follows: taking money from friends is the surest way to lose them.

But what is the alternative, especially as VCs become scarcer players in the financing ecosystem?

Angels. While VCs primarily invest other people's money, angels invest their own. An entrepreneur working on a fledgling idea needs investors who not only provide valuable business advice but who also connect the dots to make business development partnerships happen, help recruit key team members, and advance the venture from concept to fundable company. Good angels tend to have the operational background necessary to play such an active role.

In Silicon Valley, "super-angels" like Ron Conway, Reid Hoffman, Ram Shriram, and Jeff Clavier are providing seed capital and much, much more. Don Hutchison, a former Internet executive, is widely respected not only among entrepreneurs but also among VCs who often fund his companies. "Generally, I provide less money and more advisory support while attracting others to the deal as well," Hutchison says. In many ways, such contributions are a far better value proposition for entrepreneurs, especially those taking their first swing in the game. During the adolescence of my own career, having such mentors to shepherd me forward was invaluable. One of them, David Chen, I met over dinner one night, and explained my product idea on a napkin. From there Dave sat on two of my boards, and has remained a lifelong friend and trusted advisor.

There are even formal efforts to institutionalize angel financing: the dinner club investment group, the Band of Angels, is the best organized in Silicon Valley. Once a month, entrepreneurs are invited to pitch to the group, following which those investors interested in the venture directly engage the team. Others are following suit. Some angels have even started to institutionalize their investments by raising small funds focused on seed-stage capital. Jeff Clavier's new seed-only fund has breached $12 million. Dave Whorton's, $50 million. Stewart Alsop, a former VC from NEA, has raised a $75 million fund to invest in similar early-stage deals.

However, cracks are developing in the angel ecosystem. Super-angels have adopted a spray-and-pray strategy, spanning so many deals that their attention to each shrinks by the day. And individual entrepreneurs are once again left without the mentorship so crucial to success.

In other parts of the world, seed investment itself remains a huge barrier to entrepreneurship. In India, entrepreneurs are severely hindered by the lack of "mentor capital." They plow at business ideas without the expert guidance that can save months, even years of misdirection. A few small funds have come together to address the gap, including Mahesh Murthy and Praveen Gandhi's Seed Fund. But entrepreneurs in India still lack a route to access the many successful Indians in Silicon Valley who have the expertise to offer mentoring, connections, and capital. Unfortunately, this bridge, as of yet, is wobbly at best.

So, as entrepreneurs, especially first-timers, look to the "real" VCs, willing not only to take risks but to invest their mentoring time. Look beyond today's big venture names, and instead look to the small venture capitalists or the angels who can and will engage with you on a regular basis.

Look not simply for capital, but mentor capital.

Fund Envy

There was no shortage of cheers on Sand Hill Road when Foundation Capital announced in 2008 a new $750 million fund, of which $250 million was allocated for the capital-intensive cleantech sector.

However, it made my heart sink. There went another strong early-stage venture firm. For how can you practice true venture capitalism if you have to put so much money to work? It is, nonetheless, the latest trend. Venture capital firms are raising more and more money, limiting their investments to later-stage companies. NEA's current fund is one of the largest at $2.5 billion. So large it makes the term "venture capital" sound ridiculous!

Paul Kedrosky, a venture capitalist and author of the blog "Infectious Greed" disagrees with me over the implications of these monster funds. He writes, "a) I have no problem with Foundation raising a big fund to do cleantech b) there is oodles of money at both Series A and angel, and c) most angels are clueless. Then again, most VCs are clueless, so that's not news." I can only agree tepidly with his third point. Yes, many VCs and angels are clueless. But that means those with a clue must be preserved.

Foundation Capital is a great example of a firm with solid operational talent. Its general partners – Bill Elmore, Paul Koontz,

Paul Holland, Mike Schuh, and Warren Weiss – have all held senior executive positions in workaday companies. "Each of us left successful careers in industry to work in venture capital," their story goes, "because we wanted to pursue our passion: working with other entrepreneurs to build great new companies." And Foundation knows how to do just such early-stage venture capital – its partners can put out a few phone calls on behalf of a young entrepreneur and make the difference between success and failure. They can get immediate call-backs from top 500 corporate CIOs. For a fledgling idea their support is a key to the city. But fledgling and $750 million rarely go hand in hand.

In the past, if solid VCs didn't think you were ready for the big time, but that your technology was still interesting, they had the marketing savvy to help you reposition your venture in order to solve a different problem than what you had set out to. This is why entrepreneurs flock to VCs: coaching, contacts, and other unquantifiable attributes still abundant in Silicon Valley. But entrepreneurs, I bring bad news: today's leading VCs rarely extend the expertise on your behalf. They'll do things just as easily done by bankers – namely, manage money.

Why? Foundation's nine general partners now manage this $750 million fund, plus the remnants of a $525 million fund raised two years ago. As venture funds typically run a 7- to 10-year life cycle, the earlier fund is presumably still sitting around, largely uninvested. Management fees for venture capitalists are 2.5% of capital. That means with just the $750 million, Foundation Capital is already taking in $18.75 million per year. Now add the fees still rolling in from the previous fund, another $13 million and change per year. Per my back-of-the-envelope calculations, the general partners are taking home an average of $2.5 million per year – before incentives. When the general partners' investments start actually generating returns, they get paid 20–30% of the profits, otherwise referred to as the carry.

Now, apply the formula that I explained above to various fund sizes, and see what you get. If your fund is $100 million, you only get paid $2.5 million a year in management fees. Split that among, say three general partners, pay for office space, some analysts and secretaries – each partner takes home a reasonable paycheck, but hardly enough for a private jet. It isn't hard to see why successful VCs are reaching for the easy money of bigger and greener pastures.

The rule of thumb in venture capital is for each partner to manage $50 to $75 million in capital, handling an average of five to eight deals at any given time. This equation gets very complicated in the seed and early-stage game. Managing those investments involves more work, including shepherding young entrepreneurs through the learning curve that every new venture requires.

And for all this heavy lifting? The promise of sweet and easy returns not to early-stage investors, but to those who invest later. The real money is in Series B. So there too have gone the real (and rare) VC talents. For greed, indeed, is infectious.

BOOTSTRAPPING,
MONTANA STYLE

Greg Gianforte does not believe in raising money from investors. "The best money comes from customers, not investors," the former Silicon Valley software entrepreneur says.

Gianforte had to believe that. After selling his first startup to McAfee for $10 million in 1994, he moved to Bozeman, Montana, and launched another software company. But getting funding for RightNow, his new customer-service software company, proved impossible – Bozeman wasn't the tech hotbed or venture capital magnet he'd come from.

"All my business contacts literally threw away my card," Gianforte recalls. "They thought I was finished when I made the decision to start a company headquartered in Montana." Thank goodness Gianforte believes in bootstrapping; there was no other way to get RightNow off the ground. He plowed $50,000 of his own money into the company and did all the work himself – from cold-calling companies to training them on how to use the software, which lets customers get answers to questions in a Web-based FAQ. Remember, this was 1997, when Web-based automated customer service was just getting started.

Once Gianforte got a sense that he could sell the product himself, he hired three sales reps who worked entirely on commission. To further slash RightNow's burn rate, he decided against paying himself a salary. Cash was being preserved at all costs, a golden rule of bootstrapping.

Before long, RightNow's revenue was doubling every three months. Two years in, with 150 employees and $6 million in revenues, the company was valued at an astronomical $130 million. Gianforte finally raised venture capital. In two rounds – the first in 1999 and the second in 2000 – RightNow raised $32 million from Greylock and Summit.

When RightNow went public in 2004, the management team owned 70% of the company. Today Gianforte still owns 28% of the company, which crossed the $100 million mark in revenues in 2006 and today boasts a market cap close to $500 million.

How was he able to keep such grip on the reins? Bootstrapping offers entrepreneurs tremendous leverage with late-stage VCs. In early-stage venture capital funding, much of the power and control lies with the investor; in later stage funding, entrepreneurs often call the shots, with VCs falling all over themselves to offer up money.

What I find even more compelling about Gianforte's story is that it proves that distributed economic development remains possible in America. As India's engineering and customer service workforce becomes more expensive, it is in places like Montana and Wyoming that companies can find viable alternatives to support their growth. Even though Bozeman is no Silicon Valley, Gianforte says RightNow has had no problem attracting high-quality engineers. In fact, he managed to lure many away from Silicon Valley – an advertisement in a San Francisco paper garnered some 2,500 resumes. After all, salaries may be lower in Montana, but so is the cost of living. And even an engineer will admit that fly-fishing and skiing trump traffic congestion and rumbling airplanes overhead.

Just as I think India needs to find second- and third-tier alternatives to the seven major metros – Bangalore, Mumbai, Delhi, Hyderabad, Kolkata, Chennai, and Pune – America needs to do the same. Unlocking, as Gianforte has done, the still untapped potential of the American hinterlands.

GREG GIANFORTE, RIGHTNOW

The first time I sat down with Greg Gianforte in his modest San Mateo office, I knew I'd found a kindred spirit. The CEO of RightNow is a hardcore right-wing capitalist, and like me, believes that entrepreneurship is the solution to the world's economic problems. But even more precisely, Greg is so concerned about the obsession among entrepreneurs to raise external capital that he wrote a bootstrapping book to teach his hard-learned tricks.

And tricks, he has no shortage of. Industry observers say that RightNow's early product left a lot to be desired. There were other, superior products in the market from companies swimming in venture capital. However, Greg managed the last laugh, refining his product over time, while maintaining financial control of his company, and his destiny.

SM: To start, let's talk about your background. GG: I'm an engineer. My undergraduate degree is in electrical engineering and my master's is in computer science. I attended school at the Stevens Institute of Technology in Hoboken, New Jersey.

SM: Can you give us some background on Brightwork?
GG: Brightwork was a company I co-founded to develop network management applications. It was founded in 1986 in a sunroom in New Jersey. We developed tools focused on the Novell Netware solutions, since they were the dominant player back then. Ultimately we sold the company to McAfee for about $10 million, hence the Montana retirement before RightNow.

SM: The network market was chaotic at that time. How did you break through as a bootstrapped company? GG: We had a good product for Novell Netware environments. But sales were terrible. We didn't have a reputation, so nobody would talk to us. We knew we had to leverage somebody else's credibility to break into the market, we just weren't sure how.

Since Novell was the dominant player in the market, and our product focused on the Netware environment, we figured with their endorsement we could get a solid foothold. Since we didn't know how to get their attention, we decided to buy a 48-foot-long billboard across from their corporate headquarters. Novell was headquartered in Provo, Utah, and billboards there didn't cost too much. I think it was $200 a month, including lights.

The billboard had eight-foot-high letters that read, "Don't just network, Brightwork." The very next day we received a phone call from the senior vice president of communications at Novell asking for our PR department. My partner had answered the phone, so he put his hand over the receiver and asked if I wanted to be the PR department. He passed the phone over, and I picked it up and said, "PR department."

I asked what prompted the call and the reply was, "A billboard you have in front of our building. We're trying to figure out who you guys are." To which I replied, "Where are you located?" The answer, of course, was Provo, Utah. I said, "You mean those marketing people put one in Provo, too?" We ended up flying out to meet with Novell, and we left with a distribution deal. All of this occurred in just six weeks.

We shipped $100,000 worth of our product to them, which they put in their warehouses. Two months later they tried to return it; fortunately our contract did not allow them to do so. From that point on we were able to use the fact that Novell was distributing our product as a point of credibility when calling banks and larger corporations around the country. It gave us the start we were hoping for.

SM: **What were your revenues at Brightwork?** GG: Ultimately it grew to $10 million a year in revenues.

SM: **Nuggets of knowledge you took away from Brightwork?** GG: Brightwork was my first entrepreneurial endeavor, and I had a steep learning curve. I remember very early on looking for mentors to help me understand business. I think every family has somebody who's the "business expert," and mine was no different. Uncle Pete was the one in our family everybody said I had to talk to. He gave me a bunch of advice, which I went off and used. About a month later I came back for more advice because I thought what he had given me was really useful. This time he said, "Greg, you're pouring your heart and soul into this thing; I hope they're taking care of you." I didn't realize he had always been in big business. He had a completely different frame of reference, and it was not appropriate for entrepreneurial startups.

> *That was my big lesson from Brightwork: find an entrepreneurial mentor, and if you're going to bootstrap, find a mentor who has already bootstrapped a business.*

SM: **What was your exit from Brightwork?** GG: McAfee acquired Brightwork. At the time we were 50% larger than they were.

SM: **Why were they interested in purchasing Brightwork if they were in the security market and you were in the net-**

working market? GG: At the time, McAfee owned about 67% of the antivirus market compared with Symantec, which had 14%. They were interested in leveraging our sales channel since we had good relationships with network managers and a strong telesales process. McAfee had been selling to very large customers like the government and Ford Motor Corp. They realized they were going to need to start expanding their sales channels in order to maintain their market lead and continue growth. They also needed to change their sales approach, and we had a proven telesales approach that worked.

SM: Your sales methodology at Brightwork was telesales? GG: Initially, yes. We had a very viable model financially. We hired telesales people, and they would be profitable in 30 days. By that I mean we hired them, trained them, and within 30 days they were covering their costs. We hired sales individuals in classes of five every month until we had 75 people selling.

SM: How long did it take to hire those 75 people? GG: That occurred over an eight-month period. We also did it organically; we didn't use external financing to fund the growth.

SM: How did that transition to McAfee? GG: At McAfee we had 300,000 people a month downloading our software. At the time we were the most profitable software company in the world on a percentage basis. The year I started there, it was 72% pre-tax profit. Our job in sales was to get the pirates to pay us. It was really profitable, largely due to our strategy of giving it away and then tracking down the big violators of our licensing agreements.

SM: Can you quantify the results in terms of revenue? GG: When McAfee bought us they had $25 million in revenues. A year later they had $60 million. It was a combination of telesales and Web sales, but it was largely based on what we did at Brightwork. We were even selected by *Fortune* as one of the "10 Coolest Companies in America" because of our sales approach.

SM: What came after Brightwork and McAfee? GG: I retired to Bozeman, Montana in 1995. I used to vacation in Montana when I was a kid. I did some backpacking trips there. I decided to retire there because I thought it would be a good place to raise my family. We ended up buying a house outside of Bozeman with a good amount of land. It was a lot of fun at first with all the camping and fishing, but it just wasn't enough. I didn't want my tombstone to be: Dedicated to Fishing! I had the talent for starting companies, and I felt that it was unethical for me to waste that talent. So, I decided to create 2,000 high-paying high-tech jobs in town. I launched an incubator and started mentoring local entrepreneurs. Eventually, I decided I really needed to start another venture, which was RightNow. That company has about 700 employees now, so it's almost halfway to the goal of 2,000.

SM: What is the story of RightNow? GG: We're a SaaS company – our applications are delivered on a hosted basis. We've had eight straight years of revenue growth and a successful IPO. I think it's a good success story.

SM: Can you walk me through the founding and startup phase?

> GG: *I started RightNow in an extra bedroom in my house in 1998 with $50,000 cash.*

I had a crazy idea that the Internet was going to change how companies communicated with their customers. Consumers used to communicate about products with retailers, but when the Internet came along they started going directly to the companies. Dealing with this increase in direct consumer communication was going to increase costs for companies. I wanted to see if there was a business I could create to solve that problem.

SM: Can you tell us more about the bootstrapping elements of RightNow? GG: Confucius said you are never in a position to learn until you are totally confused. When I make presentations I tell people there's a process of immersion that's required, and that's where I started. Immersion is done by making a lot of phone calls, so I started by calling companies and asking if the Internet was changing the way they dealt with their customers. What I heard, and I heard it over and over again, was that they were having a hard time dealing with all the e-mails and inquiries they were getting because the distribution channels were collapsing.

When I asked companies how they were going to handle it, the answer was that they were going to hire more people. So I came up with the idea of putting dynamic questions on a Web site which allowed customers to help themselves. It didn't require any special software. I wrote down a couple ideas that I thought companies would be interested in buying, and started making calls. I asked, "If we had a product that allowed us to put questions and answers on your Web site, and this product would make all the e-mails go away, would you buy it?" Now here's a good lesson in bootstrapping: I did all of this before I had a product. When I asked if they would buy it, they said no. Better to find that out early on! I then asked companies why they said no, wrote their answers down, and moved on to the next phone call.

> *This was an iterative process that took about 400 phone calls to complete, but when I was done I was able to hone in on an initial product.*

In just one month, which is how long it took me to make those 400 phone calls, I knew exactly what customers would buy. That's when I went and built the initial product, in just 45 days, because

I didn't have to build a huge application, just the pieces I knew customers wanted.

Our first customer was PictureTel, followed by Time Warner. They paid us almost nothing – I think it was $250 a month. It didn't matter to me; at that point you just have to get the cash started somehow.

SM: Indeed. How did you conduct sales at RightNow?
GG: Primarily through telesales, which was combined with Internet-based demonstrations and trial periods of the product. I couldn't afford a phone switch, so we put in separate 1-800 numbers to each person's desktop. By the way, we eventually got a phone switch that we bought used off the Internet. I used to joke around that a new phone switch wouldn't give us a better sounding dial tone.

SM: No, it wouldn't! How did you approach companies? Did you sell to mid-level managers or senior executives? GG: I had no trouble finding companies that did a lousy job of serving customers over the Internet. Most had a Web site with a button that said "Click here for customer service." Back in 1998, I could click on that and find a phone number. Who goes to a Web page hoping to dial a phone? Nobody, but companies didn't know any other way to work!

My sales reps would search the Web, find customer service numbers, call up the customer service department, and tell them, "I've been on your Web site, and I have a suggestion for how you can improve service for your customers." The rep in the call center couldn't handle that type of request and would transfer the call to their supervisor. Our sales rep then talked directly to the supervisor and told them we had a way to help them improve service. We then approached sales on a trial basis. We let companies try it for a while to see if they liked it, because in order for us to do business they had to recognize the value. Typically, we eliminated 50–70% of the e-mails coming into the business.

> *So when we came a month later to shut down the trial application, the companies would say, "No! Where do we sign?"*

SM: What was your growth like? GG: In 1999 we did about $440,000 the first quarter. The second quarter we did $697,000. By the third quarter things had really picked up. We did $1.5 million in the third quarter and $3.3 million in the fourth. In 2000 we did $25 million. We passed $100 million in 2006, and we were one of the top IPOs of 2004. We beat Google in total appreciation in percentage basis, although we don't have their market capitalization.

What I like to emphasize is that we doubled revenue and the number of employees every 90 days for three years without outside funding. This is because of our sales process. I hired six salespeople before I hired the first engineer. I had 30 salespeople before I hired someone for marketing. Sales are the lifeblood of a business, period.

SM: True, but in this case, you were playing the role that a good product marketer would play. Not all entrepreneurs know how to do that. They should, though. GG: I say this a lot:

> *In war there are only two jobs: making bullets and shooting bullets. In business there are only two jobs: making the product or service, and selling the product or service.*

Every other function in the business supports those activities in one way or another. That's why we waited so long to create a marketing department. In my mind, a marketing department should provide sales tools, shorten sales cycles, and develop leads. At RightNow we were going to the companies we wanted, reaching the people we wanted, and making the deals we wanted.

It is important for bootstrappers to know exactly what marketing can and cannot do. Why organize a focus group to ask prospective customers if they would buy a product, when you could just as easily go ask them yourself and build those all-important, one-to-one relationships at the same time? Contacting prospective customers doesn't cost anything, and when you're finished you either have a stack of orders or know what will get you a stack of orders. If no one wants to buy your product, then you've learned quickly and relatively inexpensively that you didn't have a viable business idea.

SM: Is there any particular market segment that you've targeted, or do you simply focus on companies by size? GG: We have about 1,800 clients who tend to be larger organizations. Over 60% of our business is with corporations that have over $1 billion in revenue. Some of our larger verticals are telecommunications, which accounts for 19% of our revenues, and technology, which accounts for 17%. We also earn 14% of our revenues from government agencies and educational institutions, 13% from consumer products companies, 8% from financial and insurance, and 6% from both manufacturing, and travel and hospitality. We don't have a single client that accounts for more than 10% of our revenues, so our client base is diversified and distributed. This goes a long way to showing our strength as a company.

SM: You sell on a software-as-a-service model, so I'm assuming you have monthly or annual fees and do not offer perpetual licenses? GG: We did have some perpetual licenses, but those were discontinued in 2007. We're now a SaaS model with a two-year time-based agreement. Customers don't have an obligation to continue service; however, this has not been a problem. We've been growing very strong.

SM: Can you name some of your clients? GG: Sure. Medicare, Motorola, Black and Decker, Briggs and Stratton, and Nikon are some examples. They are big organizations with a focus on the consumer.

SM: How long is your sales cycle? GG: It typically ranges from 60 to 180 days.

SM: I know you've expanded into CRM. Could you identify your main products and discuss how they correlate to your annual revenue? GG: Our CRM solution accounts for about 80% of our revenue. We've expanded this tremendously over the years. RightNow Service provides an integrated, multi-channel customer service capability that captures customer interactions across traditional and online channels. This is the product we have evolved from the initial days, and we have now developed patents on this technology.

We now have RightNow Marketing, which is designed to deliver the functionality needed to manage multi-channel, multi-stage marketing campaigns. It automates standard campaign activities, optimizes resources, and leverages the information captured in sales and service interactions.

Another product we've developed along the way is RightNow Sales, which simplifies the sales process so that sales organizations can more easily manage accounts, track leads, organize contacts, and basically sell more, all while leveraging the customer information that's already in the common platform.

SM: Are all of these products sold via your sales force, or have you now developed partnership programs? GG: We do have strategic partnerships, which is our indirect channel revenue. At the end of 2007 we had 63 partners in our worldwide partner program.

SM: Can you disclose who some of them are? GG: They include folks like West Corporation, Lockheed Martin, and Convergys. We also brought on IBM in 2007.

SM: Is your market based solely in the US, or do you serve an international market as well? GG: We have a significant international market, which is growing. International sales accounted for 26% of revenue in 2006, and 29% in 2007. We plan on having continued growth in international markets.

SM: Have you taken any venture capital funding with RightNow, or has it been solely bootstrapped? GG: We raised about $27 million in 1999 and 2000. The first key is that our partners were really good. We also were a good size; we had about 160 people on board. We had a $6-million-a-year business, and they gave us a $130 million valuation. On those terms, I would probably raise money again today.

SM: You did two rounds, then? One in 1999 and one in 2000? GG: Yes, we raised $15 million in 1999, and $12 million in 2000. In both rounds we used Greylock and Summit.

SM: By waiting as long as you did, you were able to gain a great valuation. Did you also maintain a significant portion of ownership in the company? GG: I still own about 28% of the equity, and 70% of the equity was owned by the employees of the business when the company went public.

SM: You frequently caution people against taking venture capital. Why? GG: I definitely discourage venture capital in the beginning of a business because it provides a false sense of security. If you have too much money in the company, it removes spending discipline. During the startup stages an entrepreneur should be focused on customers, not on raising money.

SM: Let's move on and talk about your book. What are the core principles of bootstrapping? Why should people bootstrap? GG: If you get a bunch of MBAs together and ask them how to start a business, they'll tell you to write a business plan, raise money, and then start a bonfire and pitch the money on the bonfire. Hopefully there's a company there before the money is all burned.

Bootstrapping is how most entrepreneurs in the country start businesses. There are hundreds of thousands of businesses started in the US every year, and fewer than 1% raise money from venture capitalists or professional sources. That kind of begs the question: What did the other 99% do? I think they bootstrapped.

> *Bootstrapping is a discovery process. Rather than building an ark, waiting for animals to come, and hoping the tide rises — you take an incremental approach and discover a legitimate, real-world value proposition.*

That means you only have to build a product that customers will actually buy. I also like bootstrapping because it forces you to start the sales and learning process sooner. The only activity in an early-stage bootstrapping company is selling.

SM: You can only sell what you know you can deliver. GG: Absolutely. You don't want to mislead anyone, but there's nothing wrong with asking for money because that's how you really determine market demand. If you just pick up the phone, within a few days you'll know if you have a stupid idea or a good one. Bootstrapping accelerates your time to market, which means you start making money faster.

SM: Not only that, but it keeps you in touch with reality, whereas if you have loads of venture capital you can get complacent. GG: It's hard to have a false sense of security with bootstrapping. The mantra of a bootstrapper is, "There is always another way," because if there isn't, then you won't have any money!

That changes when you have VC money.

> *Not only is there a false sense of security, but when you raise money you take on a new set of masters. When I start a new business the only master I want is my customer.*

I believe entrepreneurs get pushed out of businesses by financial backers because the market timing isn't right, or the strategy was wrong.

It's hard to make a fatal mistake in business when you don't have money. Having venture capital masks the hard questions about business viability. If you don't have VC funding behind you and you need to put food on the table, then you're forced to figure out how to find another customer. I think that's a good thing. I think that's business.

SM: In your opinion, what are some of the typical misconceptions entrepreneurs tend to have? GG: I think the biggest problem is they think they have to have a perfect product before they can go to market. The reality is that learning does not start until you have some value proposition. When you go through the process of selling a product before you actually have a product, you learn a lot about the wants and desires of your target customer base.

Another problem is that entrepreneurs fail to immerse themselves. You have to figure out who your customers are, and spend time with them. You have to know their industry. When you think you've figured out the solution to their problem, go back and ask them for money. Do not say, "If I had this would you buy it?" Say, "I will do this for you, and I want you to write me a check." When they say no, then the learning begins. You take their input and modify your product concept, then call the next person on the list. This is an iterative process you do until companies start writing checks. The key is not to promise something you can't deliver in eight weeks. Find the feature that delivers critical value. Once you have your customers' commitment, go build it.

I also think a lot of entrepreneurs don't know the equation of business. That's sad. The equation of business is simple: Income – Expenses = Profit. You cannot influence profit directly. You can only influence income and expenses. Your value proposition to your customers needs to revolve around income or expenses.

SM: One of the things that stood out to me when I read your book was your discussion of the "Art of Thrift." Would you mind going over that for my readers? GG: The first myth is, "I need an office to impress my clients." I don't agree. If you're bootstrapping, you need to spend your money where it can make a difference. Unless you're an accountant or a lawyer, your office is not going to make you money.

Second, don't get caught up in the "I need a really expensive IT system" idea. You can go a long way with used computers, open source software, and hard work.

The third myth is, "I have to pay full price for phone bills." You might be surprised what types of discounts you can get if you ask. You can go out and buy calling cards if the phone companies won't give you a break.

The fourth myth is related to the third. A lot of people think they need an expensive phone system. You don't! You need something that meets your needs, and nothing more. The dial tone does not sound any better on a more expensive phone system.

Fifth, a lot of entrepreneurs think they cannot afford a salesperson. The real question is, "How can I employ someone for nothing?" My first employee at RightNow, Marcus Bragg, was only offered a commission structure. The thing is, he was selling a product that we knew the market wanted.

The final myth is, "I am too small to ask for a discount." That is not true. Call large suppliers and ask for a deep discount. If they turn you down they will do it nicely, so what's the harm? If they say no, then ask them what performance level you need to reach before you get a discount.

SM: You have said many times that business is not just about money. Can you comment on that? GG: It used to be that if you asked kids what they wanted to be when they grew up, they would say they wanted to be a fireman, policeman, or an astronaut. Today all they say is, "I want to be rich." I think that's really sad. Greed is not a virtue.

> *There is nothing wrong with making money, but I believe that when you build a business you need some form of higher purpose in the work you do.*

SM: Would you describe it as an ethical value proposition? GG: If you want to describe it that way, yes. At RightNow we help companies serve their customers. I think every one of us is given certain skills, and ultimately we'll be held accountable for how we use those skills. Here in Bozeman the average salary of our employees is $50,000. That's more than double the average salary in the community. I think that's a great accomplishment that resulted from my ability to build a business.

SM: Congratulations, on many levels! This has been an incredible story, and I look forward to watching your company's progress.

Getting Started with Little or No Capital

PASSION AND LEVERAGE

By now, readers know my bias toward entrepreneurs who achieve more by raising less money. Few have done it better than Cree Lawson, founder of Travel Ad Network, and Beatrice Tarka, founder of Mobissimo. Both have built substantial revenues with very little investment, heavily leveraging each of their company's first round of investment.

New York City–based Travel Ad Network is the largest Vertical Ad Network in travel. At a time when text ads were all the rage, TAN differentiated itself by pioneering graphical advertising that enhanced ad quality and profitability for both publishers and advertisers.

Today, TAN reaches users across 50 Web publishers, including Lonely Planet, Kayak, Rand McNally, Groople, and many others. Top TAN advertisers include American Express, Vacations To Go, Best Western, and Netherlands Tourism. All told some 14.4 million unique monthly US users visit the sites on its network, with a total of 22.5 million worldwide. Not bad for a company who from its inception in 2003 took no outside money until 2007. TAN closed a $15 million Series A round led by Rho Ventures and Village Ventures in April 2008, giving the company an estimated $50 to $75 million valuation.

Beatrice Tarka tells a similar story. Italian and Polish by birth, the French national has leveraged her international background and passion for travel and technology to build the vertical search engine company, Mobissimo.

Since its launch in October of 2003, San Francisco–based Mobissimo has created a staunch following of "MobiFans." With a sweet spot in international travel, it has been very successful catering to this niche that other travel sites have largely neglected.

Mobissimo indexes a large number of low-cost airlines, such as JetBlue, EasyJet and Ryanair, alongside online travel agencies and consolidators, including Lessno, Lastminute.com, and Travlguru. But what exactly gives Mobissimo its edge? Its search tool, One-Box Search, lets users enter their full itinerary in one search field instead of laboring through several online forms. A user types in the departure city, destination, and travel dates – i.e., "Mumbai to San Francisco December 21–28" – directly in the search field. "You can type any combination you like, and you don't have to know the airport abbreviation to launch your search," Tarka says.

Tarka and Mobissimo's other co-founders plowed their own money into the company while developing the technology and early business model. In April 2004 they received a little over $1 million in venture capital from Index Ventures, Cambrian Ventures, and Benhamou Global Ventures. Mobissimo's revenues have now crossed $10 million, and the company has been profitable since receiving the VC infusion.

The online travel market, expected to top $128 billion in revenues by 2011, has numerous niches attracting a glut of entrepreneurs. Besides Lawson and Tarka, several other entrepreneurs are also bootstrapping travel startups, including Virtual Tourist founder J. R. Johnson whose story you'll read later in this volume. What I like about these startups is that they are building negotiating leverage for themselves, as evidenced in the $75 million Series A valuation that Travel Ad Network received.

Late-stage money will always be abundant in the venture capital market, but good, fundable deals are relatively rare. Entrepreneurs can even cash out a portion of their holdings in a private transaction at a strong valuation, if they choose to bring VCs in later in the game. And some startups, such as competitors Kayak and SideStep, discussed in Volume One, have banded together and done a roll-up.

Given the state of the global economy, with unemployment at a stunning 8.1% in the US, and growth slowing in China and India, it is essential for entrepreneurs to create new businesses to rejuvenate the once bullish system. These niche online travel businesses highlight a market segment where entrepreneurship is active and not dependent on venture capital to get itself off the ground. We need more such segments – and many more entrepreneurs playing in them. Just as Beatrice Tarka has capitalized on her wanderlust in developing Mobissimo, other entrepreneurs need to follow their own passions – whether that be knitting, as evidenced in Laura Zander's Jimmy Beans Wool, or dog seats, brought to market by Glen Malmskog's Saki Seat.

CREE LAWSON, TRAVEL AD NETWORK

I don't remember how I ran into Cree Lawson. On the Internet, all sorts of random introductions take place. Cree requested to speak with me, so I took the call, and immediately found myself delighted with his masterful storytelling. Travelers often develop unique perspectives and, if we're lucky, no less unique ways of expressing them. Being an avid traveler myself, Cree certainly captured my imagination with his tale of car stereos, blood, frugality, and mentors.

SM: Cree, please tell us about your personal background.
CL: I guess I'm the product of suburban America, circa 1980 – a time when there really wasn't anything more to life than contact sports, loud music, and the knowledge that the Russians really were coming at any moment. At least that's all I knew. When I wasn't dreaming, reading, or knocking the crap out of my friends on a field behind the school, you'd find me cleaning floors at cookie stores and pet shops to buy parts for my exceptionally loud car stereo. Yeah – I was that guy. At one point my stereo was worth more than my car, in fact. But the car was only worth $1,000, so that wasn't hard to beat.

There was nothing wrong with the suburbs of Nashville in the '70s. In fact, it was a good time. Johnny Cash and Roy Orbison would occasionally come to the football games and famous songwriters were always around, sometimes even sober. But my parents were never happy unless we were on the road.

> *My parents are community college teachers, so the high point of my childhood was summer. And summer meant traveling. By the time I was 18, I'd seen over 40 states – most of them from the backseat of a lime green Dodge Colt station wagon.*

We were campers. The only thing more important than sports, reading, and loud music was traveling. I only really thought about money when the tent was broken and we couldn't find a hotel we could afford.

I really didn't excel at anything except sports, dreaming, and blowing out my eardrums until I went to Belmont University on a cross country scholarship. I won a few awards for sports reporting and writing in the college newspaper, and by the time I was a senior, I was running the paper's 32-person team. Then the Internet hit. In late December 1993, the *Belmont Vision* was the fifth college newspaper to go completely online. It came out before the print version. The only thing I couldn't get online – ironically – was the ads.

After college I was a business reporter for the *Nashville Banner* for about two years before I accepted a fellowship to NYU's Center for Publishing. I came to New York and found my way to a job at *Fodor's Travel Guides*, writing them a business plan to put online advertising on their site in 1997. They didn't listen. I went on to be a business editor on the Associated Press Web site and an online marketing manager at Time Warner. Enter the Internet again. In 1999 I joined Bookface – a San Francisco–based startup that featured complete book content in browser-based reading experience supported by advertising. Sound like Google Print? You bet. Anyway – it closed. And so did the next startup I joined.

I didn't have good timing in those days, especially when I returned to online travel advertising in September 2001 to take a job at Rough Guides. There was no online travel advertising after 9/11. Rough Guides – the travel guidebook publisher – was kind enough to keep me on board, selling online travel advertising.

I knew we had an audience of international travel planners each considering spending $1,000–$5,000 on a trip. We just didn't have enough of them. So in December 2003, I put RoughGuides.com together with Igougo.com and four other travel Web sites run by Michael Thomas, and Travel Ad Network was born. I'd managed to aggregate an audience of one million travelers across six Web sites, and we'd hit critical mass.

SM: Where did you get the idea for Travel Ad Network?
CL: When I wrote a business plan for online advertising on Fodors.com, I knew that Fodor's had an affluent audience eager to spend thousands of dollars planning the best two weeks of their year. This is an appealing prospect to advertisers. But at Rough Guides we didn't have that reach. We had the targeting – and travel advertising is all about geographic targeting – but we didn't have critical mass of inventory for any given geography. We were, in a word, small.

So when Jim Donelley and Tony Cheng at Igougo.com asked me if I could help sell ads on their site, it occurred to me that you could get enough reach and develop a critical mass of targeting by combining the audiences of multiple Web sites. No one site in our network had enough Delaware page views to justify an ad campaign targeted to Delaware, but, as a network, we reached more people planning trips to Delaware than any other media outlet. Yes, I know what you're thinking – Delaware? But the same concept applies to Vegas, Paris, London, and all the usual suspects. But I like Delaware.

> *The Internet does three things particularly well: it collapses geographic boundaries; it demolishes barriers to entry for media companies; and it fragments audiences. We feel we're positioned to take advantage of all of those.*

SM: Doing something really fun! CL: There's a contact buzz that you get from working with travel. I truly believe that travel is evolving as a lifestyle, not just a mode of transport. In an industrial economy, wealth is the accumulation of goods. In an information economy, wealth is the accumulation of experiences – it's how you spend your time on the planet – and travel is the experience most folks spend their lives looking forward to. To be around that buzz is inspiring, especially if you're working 16 hours a day.

SM: What was the market landscape when you founded the company? CL: When we started Travel Ad Network, Google AdSense had just launched its textlink product, and everything was about textlinks and performance advertising. No one talked about users; it was all about clicks.

And the terms "branding" and "online" were not used in the same sentence.

We looked at the travel market and saw that airline and hotel inventory wasn't expanding at all, and we made the leap that in the future travel providers wouldn't want mere "heads in beds" or "cheeks in seats"; they'd want higher value customers, and branding elements were the way to attract the *right* users, not just more users.

So we went toward banners when everyone else was going toward textlinks. That opened the market up for us to walk in the door and sign on exclusive graphic advertising relationships with publishers.

Our travel focus, expertise, and targeting methods meant that we achieved three times the CPMs of other generalist networks.

SM: Describe the value proposition, including differentiation versus the rest of the market. CL: We're building the best travel audience online. Sounds preposterous, right? How could 50 Web sites representing a mix of premium sites like Lonely Planet and niche sites like EuropeForVisitors.com be a better media outlet than a massive site like Expedia?

People who visit the sites at the head of the tail, or the largest travel sites, are tire-kickers or late-stage buyers. These sites have undifferentiated "vanilla" audiences and shallow relationships with their readers. Our sites attract the seekers – the people who are really searching long, deep, and hard for the right experience. They're the ones who are going to tell a friend about their trip and take pride in discovering a new travel Web site, a new resort, or a new place.

We vet all the sites in the network based on these criteria about their audiences: 1) are they seekers; 2) are they engaged; 3) do they trust their media; and 4) are they likely to interact with advertisers. So for advertisers we're building the best travel audience online.

On a tactical level, we empower publishers and provide value to advertisers by organizing niche audiences. So if you're an advertiser, we know online travel planners better and can target them more effectively by virtue of having better targeting and more effective media than the other "generalist" competition.

If you're a publisher, we bring a higher tier of advertisers at more lucrative CPMs by virtue of our knowledge and relationships in the travel space.

SM: How big is the market? How do you calculate TAM? CL: We've reviewed a great deal of research on how large the market is for online travel advertising, and very specifically banner advertising on travel Web sites. Forrester says that online travel advertising was an $8-billion-a-year industry in 2007, growing to $24 billion by 2012. Graphic advertising – rich media, banners, sponsorships – makes up about 39–40% of interactive ad spend so, in rough terms, our addressable market is $3.2 billion in 2007, growing to $9.39 billion in 2008, if you restrict our business to strictly banner advertising. We're more than that.

This method of calculating addressable market leaves out a very important factor. The fundamental business model behind online travel distribution is shifting from a distribution model to an advertising model. For its first 10 years, online travel distribution was dominated by Online Travel Agencies like Expedia, Travelocity, and Orbitz distributing travel inventory on a revenue share model with travel providers. Disruptive Vertical Search models like Kayak/Sidestep, Mobissimo, Yahoo!/FareChase, and many others are now gaining market share rapidly, replacing the traditional distribution model. The ramifications of online travel shifting from a centralized distribution model to a distributed advertising model are profound, and the impact is hard to calculate.

Americans spent $73 billion on travel in 2006, more than 35% of e-commerce. So the addressable market, for Travel Ad Network, is the $3.2 billion that's currently spent on online travel advertising, plus the impact of online travel distribution moving to an advertising model.

Any way you slice it, we have our work cut out for us.

SM: And what is your business model? CL: As a business we operate on several business models, but the predominant model combines a rep firm's focus with a network's reach. We have exclusive graphic advertising sales representation agreements with our publishers. We take responsibility for all of our publisher's ad operations, serving, hosting, fulfillment, and collections. We take a modest commission before paying the publishers.

SM: What are your top target segments? CL: We've been called the "long tail of travel Web sites," but that's not completely accurate. RandMcNally.com, LonelyPlanet.com, WAYN.com, and AreaGuides.net are hardly long tail publishers. These are premium properties with deeply integrated advertising packages that command high CPMs. Generally speaking, most of our revenue comes from connecting large travel advertisers with niche travel Web sites.

SM: How did you penetrate the market and gain early traction? CL: Hard work and creative credit card pay-off programs. Seriously – we stayed under the radar, kept our focus, listened to clients' needs, and avoided going off a cliff chasing the next big thing every other month.

> *I don't know if you want to call it healthy skepticism or contrarian thinking, but we've avoided a lot of dead ends that were billed as "the next big thing."*

We were able to sign up a lot of great Web sites by going after the ones no one was looking at. We signed on travel publishers that had never had advertising before, ahead of ones that were with other networks.

From a market penetration perspective, we were pretty aggressive early on in going after travel advertisers. We knew we had a valuable audience, and we weren't shy about trying to shake up the agencies that just photocopied the previous year's media plan for the coming year. What got us early traction was developing the trust and reputation of our advertisers and publishers.

Once we were able to afford comScore and prove – through third-party data – that we had the largest travel information audience online – bigger than Yahoo! Travel – then we came of age as a media outlet.

We were able to build the largest travel information audience online for less than $500,000 in investment. That's something I hope all our first hires will look back on with pride.

SM: I love it! Congratulations, Cree. You're a down-to-earth guy. What stage are you at now? Revenue? Profitability?

Traffic? Users? Advertisers? Any other metrics you track? CL: We ran the company at break-even for the first three years. We didn't have a choice. All the profits went right back into the company (and a few to American Express and MasterCard). Now that we have some funding, we're hell-bent on pursuing the opportunity in front of us. We sacrificed a few hundred thousand in profits last year, but January revenues this year are four times what they were last year, and the network has nearly doubled in size.

As far as other metrics go, we reach about 10 million unique users right now. We look at that. We look at the CPMs we charge, and they've been holding steady despite bringing in much more inventory. We have just under 200 million ad impressions per month from 10 million unique US users.

We take on all of our publishers' inventory. Our sell-through rates vary seasonally, but we generally fill 55–80% of inventory. About 15% is international, so adjusted for that we sell out nearly all US inventory.

CPMs range from $7 for run of network, to $10 for site-specific, to $15 for premium sites, to $40 for front page integrated.

Our top advertisers are American Express, Vacations To Go, Best Western, Netherlands Tourism, and Tourism Australia. Publishers like Lonely Planet and Rand McNally are some of our top revenue-generating properties.

We sell all our inventory direct through our own sales force, which just crossed over to the double-digits. We've had revenues from day one, and we can regain profitability as soon as we scale back the growth, but right now there's just too big an opportunity before us.

Renewals and retention are also metrics we track.

Nothing is more expensive for a business on a personal and financial level than client and customer churn.

Failure to renew with advertisers that give you reasonable terms kills reputation and morale. Renewals are twice where they were last year. Publisher retention remains above 95% despite a few of our publishers, like Lonely Planet, being acquired in the past year.

SM: Fantastic execution! How did you finance the different phases of the company? CL: In late 2005 and early 2006 we signed on two publishers that, together, quadrupled the size of our audience. We grew the company to the maximum extent possible with all the profits we'd accumulated.

A few months later, one of those publishers left the network. We had all these new sales reps and one-third the ad inventory. I thought we had a cash crisis on our hands. I called Michael Thomas, an advisor and the founder of some of the first sites to join the network. I told him we were looking for some angel capital, and he stepped up.

As it turned out, the cash crisis I'd feared didn't arise, and we found ourselves more profitable than ever. So Michael and I applied the money with the goal of building the largest travel planning audience online. We made it there by spending only half the money we'd raised.

Michael brought a lot of industry connections and knowledge that he had accumulated over the past 10 years in being involved with countless online travel startups that he either spawned or advised. I hesitate to call Michael just an angel investor because he's been of such strategic value beyond an early-stage investor. The most important aspect of the relationship is the trusting and open-door policy we've developed. We've been through hard decisions together and countless entrepreneurial brainstorming sessions.

> *The only advice I have here is that the right relationship with an experienced operator is more important than the valuation you can achieve in fundraising.*

SM: Describe some of your team-building experiences.
CL: From the startups I was associated with before TAN, I know that team building is perhaps the most difficult aspect of entrepreneurship. You start, and it's just you, and you're alone and you're screaming at the world, saying, "You need change and I have it."

And then you convince some people. And they're usually lunatics. Wild, idealistic, un-tamable lunatics like yourself who stop at nothing to realize the vision. And the passion spreads, more of a disease or mass delusion than a business. And you attract a few more lunatics. And then you grow some more until you realize you don't know what you're doing, and you hire a few more not-so-lunatic people who know what they're doing. And you're like, "Yes – this is growing. I need more people."

But people don't scale without systems. So you create systems and organization. And the days become more predictable. And then the lunatics are like, "This isn't fun anymore" – you're slowly turning them from cavemen into librarians, and they go into revolt. And then you're trying to keep the librarians on the same page as the cavemen and persuade them of a group vision that's bigger than the sum of its parts. And that's difficult because you've got generalists and specialists and, like I said, lunatics. And then you have to put them in a room and say, "Guys, this is your company, and this is the direction we're going. It's your future; you decide how we're going to get there." And then everyone brainstorms and beats each other up, and they beat you up and some of them quit, until slowly, a new vision emerges and it is greater than the sum of its parts, and it's greater than you because it's a living, breathing, self-sustaining organism. It's a company. It's no longer you and a bunch of lunatics.

We're a company now, I'm happy to say, because we've been able to recruit people with lunatic passion but the professionalism to grow with the needs of the business.

Bob Sacco, for example, came on as our first sales rep, then evolved to sales manager. When we found ourselves with 10 sales reps and no marketers, Bob took on the challenge of creating a unified product from 50 different publishers, and he's excelled at that as well. Scott Cherkin, who signed on when we had 12 publishers and built it to 50, has risen through the ranks to oversee publisher relations and product development. Adam Humphreys and Marisa Woodbury-Wagner have all evolved way beyond the initial skill-sets and responsibilities they started with. As we've evolved and as the vision we created has gained traction in the marketplace, we've been able to attract more and more talent. Brian Silver's been an amazing new addition to the team as the COO. But we will continue to promote from within wherever we can.

SM: What is your growth strategy? CL: Growing a network is pretty straightforward. You build out the sales team, and you add more publishers. We plan to continue on these core aspects while establishing more specialization, new products, and barriers to entry. We have plenty of room for growth both in publisher audience base (there are 10,000 travel Web sites out there), and in advertiser share of wallet (we're not quite at 1% of the annual $3.2 billion in revenue). So there's no shift in strategy other than going deeper with our publishers, deeper with our advertisers, and expanding things on both sides.

On the travel side, we're seeing a volatile market when it comes to travel spending. Consumer confidence is shrinking, and discretionary travel spending tends to shrink with it, but the market is bolstered by the business travel sector and the luxury travel sector.

Eventually the trend is offset by marketers raising their rates to acquire those travelers who are in the market. We saw this in the recession of 2001 and 2002. I don't anticipate that a down market will impact the travel sector for very long because travel is becoming a lifestyle.

Perhaps the most exciting growth we're seeing is in the international markets. We expanded into the United Kingdom about six months ago, and it's already representing a double-digit percentage of our revenue.

SM: What are your thoughts about exit? CL: We've certainly had offers that would've made me a very wealthy man, or at least a guy with a very loud car stereo. But I don't think Elvis will leave the building for a long time yet.

When I started this company I knew we had a lot of broad market indicators pointing in our direction – fragmentation of media, migration of ad budgets to online, travel emerging as a lifestyle, explosion of online publishing, and a lack of barriers to entry. Still, I never really thought this would roll out to be big enough to become an IPO opportunity. I thought we'd possibly be an acquisition target by a media company that wanted to dominate the travel sector of online advertising, or a travel distributor that was surprised by the advent of advertising as a travel distribution model.

In our early days I had to be realistic: we were really only a rep firm, and rep firms don't have IPOs. But as we've realized how much easier the business gets as we scale, how effective our new products and advanced targeting are, we've begun to rethink that. If international expansion continues the way it has, and travel distribution continues to shift to an advertising model, then we might just be able to pull off the holy grail of exits. For now there's no sense exiting until we figure that out.

SM: What are some of your key learnings from this journey? CL: It's hard to know where to start. It's fun to think that an organization will grow to reflect you. Unfortunately, the way that a company reflects you is like a cloning exercise in a science fiction movie.

> *The organization captures a few of your good characteristics, but it multiplies your flaws. Nothing shatters your pride more than watching this process happen. If you hire the right people and bury your pride, you can make the organization grow to reflect the best aspects of its management, without amplifying its flaws.*

One of the things we learned early on was that it's often important to take stands on principle. We didn't pursue RSS ads or podcasting early on despite a lot of pressure to do so. Bob and I just didn't think it would work out for travel. It turns out we were right. But we also took a stand early on not to pursue behavioral targeting because we didn't think it would be as effective as contextual targeting. We were uncomfortable with the privacy issues. We thought it was just another flash-in-the-pan way to extract value from remnant inventory and a trick to get the last view through conversion. It turns out we were wrong on at least three of those four reasons. We'll see where the privacy issue sorts out. But we were standing on a principle, not listening to the market. Once we decided behavioral was essential for travel advertising, Scott Cherkin has helped us catch up to everyone else, but we were slow out of the gate, and this was a mistake based on our standing on a platitude rather than listening to the market.

On a personal level, I've learned to trust my coworkers more than I ever thought I'd be able to. And they've delivered more than I ever expected. We've all pushed each other to levels that I never thought we could achieve.

SM: Cree, this has been an absolute pleasure. I wish you the very best!

BEATRICE TARKA, MOBISSIMO

Beatrice Tarka is stubborn, hard-charging, and focused. She drills in the focus through constant reiteration of her core strategy. International. International. International. Yes, Beatrice, we got it!

If you think it's overkill though, think again. Communication is a key aspect of a CEO's job, and Beatrice Tarka leaves no ambiguity whatsoever. To customers, analysts, media, and employees, a company's positioning, strategy, and direction can have no grey area.

SM: Please describe your personal background. What was your family like, your upbringing, and your early career?
BT: I'm a would-be astronomer with a math and physics heart. My background is international and eclectic. I'm Italian and Polish by birth and French by citizenship. I grew up in Poland and learned to speak English reading astronomy books. Technology inspired me at a young age because it's an enabler of problem-solving. I credit my entrepreneurial streak and my passion for new technology, especially the Internet, to my multicultural upbringing.

My older sister works for a major international airline. As a teenager, even before PCs, I connected travel with technology. My first experience with computers was playing on my sister's office computer accessing her company's mainframe. As flights were very expensive at the time, I was running archaic SQL queries to find unpublished fares for the foreign delegations searching for cheap flight combinations.

My first experience with personal computers dates to the first ZX Spectrum where you had to load the operating system via cassette!

Later I graduated from the American University in Paris with a degree in computer science and international business. I earned my MBA on the Belgian campus of Boston University. Before bringing Mobissimo to the US, I co-founded two other software companies.

SM: What companies were those? BT: The first was Axall Media, an entertainment software publisher. The second was France Portage, a press distribution database provider, which was acquired by France Telecom.

For me the process of becoming a technologist was progressive. It evolved from playing with the mainframe, to programming, and then on to games. After that it was consumer software and finally the Internet. I've always identified that the computer can solve complex problems at great speeds. That's been the driver all along.

SM: Where did you get the idea for your current venture? Did you have prior domain experience in the travel segment? BT: First and foremost at Mobissimo we are travelers ourselves. We have felt the pain of endless attempts to search for and book tickets online.

In my prior venture I found myself traveling back and forth between the US and Europe, as well as various other places, and I was booking flights and hotels as often as a travel agent would. Scouring multiple Web sites for the best deals was anything but quick and easy. With my expertise in data extraction and aggregation, I decided to create the best travel search engine possible, the goal of which was to simplify the search process and get a better view of all travel offers.

After I had this idea I reached out to people in my sphere with technical backgrounds and travel domain expertise. I started Mobissimo with Svetlozar Nestorov, a childhood friend who was in the same group at Stanford as Sergey Brin and Larry Page. Our vision is reflected in the name, Mobissimo, which in Italian means "the ultimate in mobility."

SM: What was the market landscape like when you founded the company? BT: The emergence of ticketless booking has made a huge difference in the travel landscape. For the first time you could buy your ticket in the morning and travel in the afternoon without having to wait for, or pass by, the travel agent to pick up your ticket.

The traditional travel agent model moved online with On-line Travel Agents (OTAs) like Expedia, Travelocity, and Orbitz providing their first fare offerings to users in the late '90s. These merchants sell their inventory as a "point of sales" for participating airlines.

SM: But that is not a user friendly environment. BT: Not at all, and it got even worse. Next there was the explosion of low-cost carriers all over the world. All of this created a jungle of places to look for fares, with huge implications for the consumer. People may have known about the major airlines' fares, but they didn't have a clue about what all these new companies were offering. For the user, none of these services were comprehensive, and because of that people weren't able to quickly uncover the best rates. This is the environment where the metasearch travel comparison sites came into the game. We came into the market alongside emerging companies like FareChase, SideStep, and Kayak.

SM: What's the value proposition of Mobissimo? BT: We find the cheapest airfares and among them the best international fares. To synthesize, we simplify the search process by querying multiple Web sites in real time to deliver highly valuable information to the user. We make it easier for people to travel.

SM: What differentiates you from your competition? BT: The first differentiator is our superior platform technology. Our core search engine is our own development, not third-party technology such as Kayak's. Our technology is based on years of research experience in information extraction, integration, data mining, and search technology conducted at Stanford.

Second, we provide innovative products and features that improve the travel search experience for consumers while driving higher conversion rates for our suppliers. We pioneered OneBox Search, which is a natural language search feature that allows users to enter itinerary information directly into a single search box without filling out online forms. A user just types the departure city, the destination, and dates directly into the search field. You can do it just like this: "San Francisco to Rome March 18–28." You can type any combination you like, and you don't have to know the airport abbreviation to launch your search.

Another distinguishing feature is ActivitySearch, our theme-based travel planning tool that mirrors the way consumers think while making travel plans, revealing many more travel choices than the user may initially think of. Just enter your departure city and then pick from a category such as "skiing," "beaches," or even "wine tasting" and reserve the trip that corresponds to your budget and interests.

We also offer a targeted in-house advertising platform that allows suppliers to target audiences by destination and date. When a customer clicks on the ad, the search is performed immediately.

SM: I've noticed you have some very interesting personalization features as well. BT: In February we launched a new version of Mobissimo that allows users to personalize the way their travel page looks, and we've added travel-related content such as weather, photos from Flickr, and other destination information. It's an interface that synchronizes and updates with each user's search.

SM: Is your sweet spot in international or domestic travel? BT: Mobissimo can handle both, but the sweet spot is our international expertise. No other metasearch engine brings such a broad selection of travel suppliers simultaneously into one place, available with one click.

Today, Mobissimo is the undisputed international travel search expert because we cover more low-cost airlines such as Ryanair and JetBlue, as well as foreign consolidators like Lessno, MakeMyTrip, and Go Voyages, than our three main competitors combined. We operate six local Web sites in North America, France, the UK, India, Poland, and Spain, and we'll be expanding our offering in APAC.

SM: Makes sense. International was more of a hole in the market when you got in, and it is a lot cheaper to buy search engine traffic in Poland than in the US. Do you offer page-rank advertising to your suppliers? BT: No, we prefer to maintain objectivity. We don't charge travel suppliers to be listed in the top results of our search engine, and because of that we remain the only completely objective travel search engine. That is supremely valuable to our customers.

SM: What is your TAM, and how do you calculate it? BT: According to Henry Harteveldt, Forrester Research's travel expert, the online travel market represents the highest growing proportion of the overall travel market. Online travel is also the most lucrative. Mobissimo is focused on the larger, international, online travel market which represents $600 billion versus $225 billion for the US domestic market in 2008. That's our sweet spot.

SM: How are you earning revenue, from referrals or by commission? BT: Our business model taps into this vast, growing market through advertising revenue and referral fees, much like Google's business model. We don't tax our back-end system by getting involved in the transactions themselves.

SM: What are your top target segments? Do you have substantial traction in anything other than international travel? BT: We do support the US travel market. Although the US market is large, it's the international market that's growing exponentially. China and India are two markets that have seen incredible growth recently, as well as Eastern Europe.

Drilling down into demographics, women may be our greatest users. Sometimes it's a businesswoman or entrepreneur like yourself, maybe an executive assistant booking travel for her boss, or sometimes a young woman planning a getaway vacation from home. But women are smart shoppers who know how to find the best bargains. QuantCast numbers show that Mobissimo attracts a particular user profile. Our user demographics are slightly skewed to a female audience: 56% of our users are women; 34% of our users' household income exceeds $100,000 per year; 70% of our users have had higher education. The typical user is female, the largest group of which is aged 25–45 years old, followed by the 55 and older age group. We have a great ethnicity mix as well, representing some 200 countries, with a strong African American, Asian, and Hispanic user base. Our customer makes the travel decisions not only for him- or herself, but often for the entire family.

SM: How did you penetrate these market segments and this demographic to get early traction? BT: Mobissimo was, and is, appealing for the end user because we have content, and thus prices, that no one else has.

We display travel information for suppliers who are not accessed through traditional travel sites. This includes a large number of low-cost airlines that we alone cover. In one single place you can find over 80 low-cost airlines from around the world such as

JetBlue, EasyJet, Ryanair, Centralwings, Wizz Air, Vueling, Click-air, Spanair, Kingfisher, and Jet Airways, as well as multiple online travel agencies and consolidators like Lessno, Vayama, Airfare.com, Go Voyages, Opodo, Ebookers, Lastminute.com, Nouvelles Frontieres, Terminal A, Travlguru, and Yatra.

We went for the affluent early adopters and got good traction there.

Within a month of our launch, Time Magazine *put us on their list of the "50 Coolest Web sites," and "Mobissimo addicts" or "MobiFans" were born.*

SM: Where are you now in terms of revenue and profitability? BT: The Mobissimo.com site has been open to the public since November 2004, and we've generated revenue and been profitable since June 2005. Our revenue comes from CPA transactions and advertising revenue such as banner ads, CPM, and sponsored links (CPC). In addition to our search engine, we've developed a Mobissimo home-grown ad platform that allows our partners to target specific geographical audiences and dates. We plan to expand this highly targeted ad platform to other travel related sites.

SM: What types of metrics do you use to track progress? And how are these numbers progressing? BT: To give you more numbers, Mobissimo has relationships with more than 180 travel partners around the world, and over 200 advertisers. Among the largest advertisers are Travelocity, Starwood Hotels, American Airlines, Virgin America, British Airways, Singapore Airlines, Hawaiian Airlines, and the Bahamas Tourism Office.

We track the number of visitors, number of searches made by visitors, clicks, page views generated, and the amount of time spent on the site, as well as repeat user rate.

SM: How did you finance the different phases of the company? Did you bootstrap, take angel funds, raise rounds through VCs, or a combination? BT: We self-funded Mobissimo while we developed the technology and early business model. In April 2004 we received a little over $1 million in venture capital from Index Ventures, Cambrian Ventures, and Benhamou Global Ventures.

SM: You became profitable very fast, very early. Will you be raising more money? And if so, what type of investor is your ideal investor? BT: Since our venture raise in 2004, the company has been profitable and cash flow positive and has been growing self-sustained between 100–150% annually.

This year we see a tremendous opportunity to accelerate our growth in revenue through our international strategy, and we're considering expansion capital to help us grow at a much higher multiple. Given our financial track record, results, and profitability, we have several possibilities open including venture funding, private equity, debt equity, and even a private placement on European stock markets.

We value a partner who shares our vision of the huge opportunity in international markets that I spoke of earlier. That's a $600 billion TAM compared to a $225 billion US domestic TAM. Our ideal investor is also someone who understands that with the weak dollar and incoming recession, growth in the US market will be challenged, but that Mobissimo is the only player well positioned to continue growth through its existing network of six foreign Web sites, our upcoming foreign Web sites, our marketing and business development expertise in these markets, and finally our strong international user base. Naturally, our ideal partner would also be financially solid, have international expertise, and maintain strategic relationships in the travel sector that complement our own.

SM: Could you describe how you went about putting together your team? BT: In my two prior ventures I built strong management teams, sometimes through trial and error. This time I knew what I was looking for in terms of not only experience and background, but character and personality.

> *You can have the best technology and the best product on the market, but without good team chemistry your business will fail.*

We're lucky in that we have both.

SM: What is your growth strategy from here on out? BT: We're always working on improving our search technology and the user experience to make sure Mobissimo users find the best fares and stay loyal to us. The market grows every day, and we're growing along with it. The fact that we provide travel and booking information to parts of the world like China, India, and South America is great because we're seeing enormous growth in travel to those regions, which allows us to expand accordingly. We're the No.1 brand in international emerging markets, and our aim is to be the best international travel search brand.

In addition to having the best technology and most comprehensive site, we've pioneered recommendation tools such as our ActivitySearch, which allows users to search for theme-based travel options while offering us new forms of revenue growth.

SM: What are your thoughts in terms of a potential exit? BT: I'm not too focused on the exit. We're building a strong company and brand in a growing market, so the vision and execution is what we focus on most. I spend my time working to improve Mobissimo, whether through its technology, new partnership opportunities, or new ways to reach travelers and prospective users.

The market condition in the travel industry gives us many opportunities. Mobissimo is not a "feature," but a standalone company, thus we could go public if the financial climate and revenues were permitting. We're also one of the best types of partners to have for companies that want to grow and need international expertise in content, contacts, and marketing.

SM: What are some of your key learnings from this journey so far? BT: A solid core team and market timing are key success factors. I also have my own "6 P" concept: Passion, Product Vision, Perseverance, Pleasure (to learn, create, discover, and adapt over and over again), Progress, and Personality. If you believe in what you're doing and work hard, persevere, and never lose sight of your original vision, then you'll ultimately succeed.

SM: This has been a pleasure; best of luck to you.

BARACK OBAMA'S
FINANCE LESSON

B arack Obama wants to create American jobs, and, as he declared at the Democratic National Convention, he also wants to cut capital gains taxes for small businesses. Although his speech was stirring, reminiscent of other great orators like Kennedy and Martin Luther King Jr., Obama still exhibits a colossal ignorance on economics and small-business issues.

For starters, small businesses don't pay capital gains taxes. Furthermore, Obama plans to tax wealthy individuals and angel investors who now, more than ever, supply the lifeblood of start-ups. Such a stranglehold on entrepreneurship is precisely what he doesn't want to do.

If it weren't for wealthy individuals willing to gamble on new ventures, we wouldn't have entrepreneurs or their small businesses – the backbone of America's economy.

Take Rafat Ali. He could not have turned his moonlighting hobby, business blog paidContent.org, into a multimillion-dollar business without seed money from legendary media investor Alan Patricof. Ali founded paidContent in 2002. By 2008, the blog was generating several million dollars in advertising revenues annually.

The American landscape is dotted with variations of this story. Entrepreneurs like GigaOM's Om Malik and TechCrunch's Michael Arrington left careers as lawyers and journalists to build small businesses with their blood, sweat, and angst. Malik took initial seed financing from True Ventures, a small, relatively new venture capital firm, while Arrington funded his blog with his own money. Another former lawyer, J. R. Johnson, founded VirtualTourist.com in 1999 with $313,000 of friend's and family money before, in 2008, selling it to Expedia's TripAdvisor in a multimillion-dollar deal. The list goes on.

Hydro Green Energy chief executive Wayne Krouse is an *Atlas Shrugged* kind of guy who waited four years for a patent that would allow him to launch a cleantech company that promises to greatly enhance hydropower in the US. His friends and family – all doctors – chipped in a little over $500,000 to make his vision a reality. Today, Krouse has raised substantially more money and is on his way to building a company that creates the kind of "green" jobs Obama only dreams of.

If you read these stories carefully, much of the money that enabled the creation of these ventures came not from VCs, but friends and family, doctors, lawyers, and of course, the entrepreneurs themselves.

There is a very simple fact that Obama's socialist rhetoric misses: You have to make and have money before investing in the startup dreams of our next generation of entrepreneurs. By taxing the wealthy, Obama threatens to undermine their ability to refuel an already faltering economic engine.

To be fair, it is a complicated engine President Obama stands before. And few of its parts are working in synch. Furthermore, the president came to power on the basis of multiple socialist principles, but must now stand before his still cheering crowds and make a steady, unwavering case for the need for those who have money to be given the chance to reinvest it before it is taxed out of the market. He has to convince the Senate and Congressional

Democrats steeped in ideological mental blocks that there is truly no other way.

A staggering 8.1% unemployment rate stares America in the face. Some 35 million Americans woke up unemployed today. Their working counterparts might have hurried their breakfast this morning, but a hurried breakfast on the way to work is better than breakfast in a sinking bed.

Aim for the moon, Mr. President, even if you only reach the stars – say, five million new jobs – the American people will thank you.

Om Malik, GigaOM

Having covered technology for major publications such as Red Herring *and* Forbes, *Om Malik is, to say the least, a successful journalist. He has also been itching to be an entrepreneur for as long as I have known him, close to 10 years.*

Back then, like many pioneers, he had to move mountains to get blogs legitimized, working weekends, nights, and into the wee hours of the morning. Om is unquestionably one of the pioneers of the blogging phenomena, and with GigaOM, he is one of the first bloggers to have monetized blogs in a significant way, crossing a million dollars in revenue in 2007.

SM: I would like to start by going back to your roots, to the circumstances you grew up in. What was India like at the time? And what was your life like? OM: I grew up with what I would describe as a pretty regular middle class life in Delhi. The education was thanks to my mother, who basically made sure I studied hard. I think the American equivalent would be growing up in the Midwest, with pretty strict parents. I believe that gave me a solid grounding in what really mattered, and how one needs to go through life.

SM: Where did you go to school? OM: I went to school and college in Delhi. Somewhere down the line I got into student writing, becoming a journalist.

SM: What did your parents think about your choosing to become a journalist, as opposed to a doctor or an engineer? OM: They never opposed it, but I'm not sure they were exactly excited about it. I did feel that it was my calling. My mother and father both write very well, just not professionally. I never received opposition from them, but deep down I'm sure they worried about how I would make a living. Journalism was not exactly an incredible profession back then in India. However, you have to do what you have to do.

SM: What was your first beat in India? OM: I worked for a magazine called *VP Fun*; it's sort of like *Tiger Beat*. I would write about music, college life, inter-school music competitions, and those types of things. It didn't seem very difficult, but over the years I evolved. I did whatever I had to in order to climb the ranks.

SM: What was the first significant position you had, something you consider a milestone? OM: I don't think there's been anything that significant. I've been going through an evolutionary process – one step at a time. I think the first job was the most crucial because without that I wouldn't have had any foundation.

SM: The college music publication? OM: Yes. As I grew older, I wrote about a whole bunch of issues for a whole bunch of newspapers. Very early on in my life I went into a freelance mode and took a multi-platform approach. I wrote for Sunday newspapers, daily newspapers, and magazines because I wanted to have maximum impact. That also meant I had to work too much, but that was part of the joy of writing for so many different people. It also meant more money.

SM: **Did you go outside of India for work?** OM: I left India mostly for personal reasons. There wasn't a pressing need to leave the country; I was doing well. But for some personal reasons I realized I needed a break. Another thing I realized was that I wanted to be playing on a bigger stage. I was ambitious. I wanted to be a journalist in a big media market like New York, so I started working toward that.

SM: **But you didn't go from Delhi to New York, did you?** OM: No, I went to various places. I traveled a little through Europe. I was in London for a while, and then spent time in Eastern Europe. I got to New York after. I think it was a bit of an epiphany to be honest, but I got to New York and stayed for just a couple months. I then went back to Delhi, then came back again.

SM: **Why was that?** OM: I wasn't ready for New York. My grandmother had passed away, and something inside me was telling me something was wrong and I had to go back. My parents never told me what was wrong, but I knew instinctively that I had to go back. Then I heard she was dead. I came back to New York after a few months with a bigger plan, with everything in place.

SM: **What year was this?** OM: It was 1992.

SM: **It was before the Internet bubble had started.** OM: That was one of the things that crystallized things for me. While I was in London I had acquired a laptop and signed up with CompuServe. I read a few things about ARPANET, and it had a profound impact on how I thought and how the world looked to me at that point. I thought it would be an amazing story, and that I would try to follow that chain of thought.

SM: **Were you working for *Forbes* in New York at that time?** OM: No, I came here without a job. Basically, I came here with some freelance work.

SM: Sounds like a fairly risky move for you to go to New York at that point. OM: Yes.

> *I didn't have a plan. When you're young you're stupid, which is absolutely the upside.*

SM: Heavens yes! If you knew what you were getting into, you wouldn't get into it! OM: Exactly. That's why this whole past week I've been amazed – finally I get why Zuckerberg doesn't want to sell Facebook. What you don't know, you don't really know and it can't hurt you.

SM: When you're that young, if you don't make a billion dollars right away it's fine. OM: One of the things I always talk about is that when I got here I did some part-time work. It was not a shining moment of my life. I did some pretty hard jobs like working in grocery stores, but you can't go wrong. Even if I was only making $500 a week, it was more than I would in my entire lifetime as a reporter in Delhi. It was a little stupid and foolish, but you have to have a bit of faith.

SM: The most important thing is to have faith in yourself. OM: I don't really credit it to bravery; I think it was a little luck and a bit of a divine plan.

SM: You have to trust that divine plan. You have to trust your destiny and that your destiny is going to take care of you. You have to have the internal resources to cope with the swings you take at life. OM: I think it's easy to "Just do it" – it's not like I'm going to Congo. This is America. You can speak the language; historically this has been a welcoming place. Sure, the odds are against getting a job in a mainstream American publication, but why not?

SM: How did you manage to pull off the transition from writing for a South Indian magazine to becoming a writer at a mainstream American publication like *Forbes?* OM: I worked for a bunch of ethnic Indian newspapers in New York. Some of those gigs were not exactly satisfying. *India Abroad* was a pretty strong publication. *India West* had great editors who appreciated hard work. However, these places were not exactly happy places to work, but they toughened me up. I also went to school a bit as well to learn about fashion journalism.

SM: I had no idea! OM: I thought that was so far out in left field – abstract topics require your language skills to be very, very good. I spent two semesters doing that in the evenings after work. All of these jobs were part-time gigs, and it never really seemed that I was there.

> *It was just one step at a time, a learning process, and every day I learned something new. I read the newspapers a lot, read magazines a lot – basically I was re-educating myself. Whatever I did, it was constant re-education.*

SM: You were learning step by step. OM: I knew nobody was going to teach me, so I figured I would have to figure it out myself. I remember when I was younger, I was reading the *Wall Street Journal* where this guy, Greg Zachary, used to write. He's now at Stanford. I would read his stuff, then completely imitate it. Every story had to be like his.

I ended up getting a job at a Japanese newswire covering microcontrollers. That was the un-fun part. Nobody wanted to cover the damn thing. It was the least sexy job you could have. For me, however, it was fun. It was part of my education. I started at the basic building blocks of technology. At the end of the day it's all about the silicon, not about chatty social networks.

I have a unique view from the bottom up, and I still think like that. From there, I went to processors and saw the launch of Windows 95, the troubles at Apple, the rise of Cisco, and the emergence of the Internet as an economic phenomena. I wrote about Netscape very early on. I was naturally gravitating to all things network. The funny thing is, I didn't really know it; my mind was pushing me in that direction. That was the reason I got interested in technology – after CompuServe and reading about ARPANET in *Forbes*.

SM: How did you get involved with *Forbes*? OM: *Forbes* had a piece on ARPANET which had a really profound impact on me. *Forbes* was looking to start a Web site, to be one of the first mainstream publications to cover technology, online. Nobody knew when it was going to happen, but since *Forbes* was on CompuServe I used to read their stuff all the time. I hounded this guy, for seven or eight months, almost like a stalker, and convinced him he had to meet me because if he didn't he was going to miss the opportunity of a lifetime, or so I thought. I basically wore him down, and he met with me, and about 15 minutes later he offered me a job. The rest is history.

SM: Forbes.com was the second big opportunity? OM: I don't see the breakthroughs in terms of the publication I worked with. It's actually the editors I worked with. At the teen magazine the editor I worked with treated me almost like a son. He pushed me really hard and made me a better reporter. David Churbuck at Forbes.com was one of the best-known technology writers in the country. He didn't just write a story, he thought about strategy and analysis, and everything that went into it. Sitting with him and working on a daily basis, with five other guys, to build a brand-new Web site was fantastic.

SM: At *Forbes*, you were working for the first time in an American professional environment, right? OM: Yes. This was more like having the family touch, yet working with serious pros and people who were very serious about their craft. Not only did I get to work with David, but I also got to work with Jim Michaels, who is like the Michael Jordan of journalism. He clearly was not my boss, but he took time to teach me. That was eye-opening for me.

In 1999 I realized there was a boom going on, and I thought I should go tap in on that. I think that was the first time I made a move driven by greed, rather than logic and passion. I joined Hambrecht & Quist, Asia Pacific, and became an investment manager looking to do deals. Within three months I realized what a disaster that was for me.

SM: That moved you to San Francisco, correct? OM: Yes.

> *To be honest I think a lot of people do things for money, and it's the stupidest thing we can do for ourselves. Everybody thinks money is the answer, but it is not. What made me tick was writing; that's what I was born to do. How can you ignore your natural animal instinct?*

SM: You came to San Francisco, and how long did you last at H&Q? OM: Eight months, precisely. After that I went to work for *Red Herring*, which was great. It was another great place to work.

SM: This was right around when the market was crashing, yes? OM: I still joke with folks that when you hire journalists as VCs, the market will crash. I quit in August of 2000 and started to work for *Red Herring*. I think my first piece for them was something about the bursting of the optical bubble. I was naturally inclined to be a reporter. That was a great gig. I was writing about these things, and the market was still going gangbusters.

SM: The optical market did not crash until 2001. OM: Yes, it was interesting to be there when it did. Scams. Scandals. Rampant greed.

SM: *Red Herring* crashed as well, didn't it? OM: *Red Herring* lasted a bit. As the market started to turn down, I think it was in September 2001, just before 9/11, I got a chance to go back to New York because I hadn't felt comfortable living in San Francisco. When 9/11 happened, that delayed the decision, but I ended up going back and working for *Red Herring* from New York. I saw the magazine shrink and shrink. In February 2003, when it died, that's when *Business 2.0* hired me. The precondition was that I had to move back to San Francisco. So I decided to stop fighting my fate, and realized my destiny was to live in the Bay Area.

SM: Had you already started the blog by then? OM: The blog is actually in its sixth year now. I started it on December 13, 2001. Before that it existed as a Web site. I used to have a newsletter called *Dot Com Wallah*, and I used to send that out and post that e-mail on the blog with my resume. It wasn't really anything major at that point. My resume was my articles, but it became more interactive in December 2001. We added Moveable Type, a blogging software.

SM: You also wrote the book, *Broadbandits*, around that time? OM: I was basically working on the book while I was in New York. The timing was such that as I arrived in San Francisco it came out about two months later.

SM: By 2004 you're working at *Business 2.0,* and your blog is starting to take shape in its current format? OM: That's right. It hadn't totally evolved; it was only getting 500–800 readers a day.

SM: How did people find out about your blog? The mainstream media was certainly not talking about blogs yet. OM: I think there were a bunch of us talking about it. It was intriguing for me personally because it impacted what I was doing. I was working for a monthly magazine, but I was talking to 20 people a day. I had all of this information which was just redundant by the time the magazine came out. I thought, this is just stupid. It was ideal to put it out on the Web every day, and that was it. That was a big break-through moment for me. I would just do it, and I would send people e-mails and tell them I wrote about them. It started that whole dialogue. Most of my readers were people I wrote about – people featured in the book, people interested in the telecom scandal. From there it just grew. With a lot of work; blogging is a lot of work.

SM: Tell me about it! OM: People don't realize how much work it is. Everybody thinks you can just set up a blog and you get it going. If you want to do this seriously, it takes work. For me it got addictive. As soon as someone left a comment, I would read it.

As a journalist, it was very empowering. People could read my work and comment right away. It was a very passionate commu-nity. So, I started doing more and more of it. I'll always be a news reporter, and I cannot ever deny that, but a part of me is now a blogger. I was working for a monthly magazine, so this was an ideal fit for me. I kept the bigger stories for the magazine, but the smaller ones I published in the blog. Very early on I learned it was a conversation, not a news report.

By 2003 it was really only doing 25,000 visitors a month. But around April of 2006 something happened. I don't know what it was, but whatever it was, I started seeing the traffic dou-ble on a monthly basis. More visitors, more people. There was a story I broke about LiveJournal and Typecast merging, which helped a lot because suddenly there were a lot of non-telecom people reading it.

There was no other outlet, so I put it out there. I did more of those stories, and developed this blend of musing and blogging which is what you see on a daily basis.

In April 2006, with traffic growing, I was talking to Toni Schneider, the CEO of Automatic, the company behind WordPress, and he basically told me to start doing this full-time.

For a while, whenever I met people at an event, I would get asked when was I going to quit my day job and do this full-time. All of these people were outsiders. I could not figure out why they were saying this. One day, I went to see some friends from True Ventures, and they told me to just do it. They gave me a check, and told me to go with it. I didn't jump on it right away. I'd already started talking with a bunch of other VCs to hash out a game plan. Some thought there was a media disruption coming, and if one could turn blogging into a business there would be a way to make money from it. I had about three or four months of esoteric conversations like that. This was in 2005, and we knew the media mix would be interesting and could go into flux for a long time.

When I left *Business 2.0* in June 2006, there was no company, it was just me. I basically convinced my first employee, Katie Fehrenbacher from *Red Herring*, to come on board, and we were off to the races on July 5th. Everything has been a 100-meter sprint since.

SM: When did you sign up with Federated Media? OM: Right out of the gate. Before I even left my job I had already signed. I think it was the end of June, 2006.

SM: What was going on with FM then – they were just being founded at the time, right? OM: I have known John Battelle for a long time, and we talked about his idea and I told him I was on board. At that time, when he was putting ads on the sites, it was not a formal relationship because they were in the process of becoming a channel for bloggers.

Our paths converged, and it allowed me to focus on writing, while FM sold ads on my site. It eventually became clear that we had to plan together, and work on things together.

> *A lot of people make the mistake that when they out-*
> *source, they outsource it all. The reality is you outsource*
> *the physical function of it, but not the mental piece.*

It's still your core competence, core to your business.

As much as John and his team obsess about it, I have to think about it twice as hard. I think that's the crucial difference I have from other bloggers. I talk with the Federated sales reps two or three times a week. It's been a constant fine-tuning process. We have regular conversations so they know what works for me, what campaigns I like, and why. They understand the site, the audience, and what I'm doing. That's why they do a much more effective job.

This is part of outsourcing that's tough. It's not somebody on your payroll doing the job, and it's not out of your cost structure, but it is your business.

SM: All outsourcing works that way. If you try to do your software development somewhere else, and you don't monitor it and think it through, it's not going to work. OM: That is lesson number one. Lesson number two is that no task is bigger than you, and no task is smaller than you. Starting a startup is easy; making it work is a lot of hard work. It is an insane amount of work. I cannot imagine why people sign up for it, but I also get it. This has been the best year of my life.

I haven't slept more than three hours a day for the past 11 months. Maybe when I was in India to see my parents, but that was because of the jetlag, not because I wanted to sleep. It becomes your sole obsession. You really have to be obsessed about it. One of the things I miss is that I don't get enough time to think deeply, which is what I'm hoping to change. I'm hoping as the company evolves in the next 10 to 12 months, and management positions get filled out, I can go back to my natural state of thinking and writing more.

This is the third lesson, I guess, that while you have to do everything, you are a band-aid – not a permanent fix. You have to bring in the "A" team. I think the team part is the most important part because my whole vision is to not grow beyond 30–40 people. I want to keep the company small enough that we can all move in the same direction, at least in the near term. In the long term, who knows?

SM: When you look at the scaling of the company, what is your vision? Where do you want to take it? OM: I want Giga Omnimedia to be a proper publishing company. Just like companies who publish magazines and newspapers, we publish a Web/blog hybrid. Just think of it as another publishing company. We're going to take advantage of Moore's Law and do things cheaper, faster, and better. There is no rocket science.

SM: So you're thinking of a series of Web sites? OM: Right. We're up to four now, and there will be two more before the end of the year. From there it should be one every two months.

SM: What kind of traffic do these sites get? OM: We're doing 100,000–200,000 on some of the smaller sites, and the newer sites are still growing. They're all growing at a fairly rapid clip. About 20% a month. I don't look at the spikes, I look at the baseline which shows anywhere from 10–20% growth. A lot of it has to do with the market being back. Technology is back.

Another thing is we're creating value-added, high-quality content, not just pointing links or random stories. The focus is clearly on quality not on quantity. That message seems to resonate very well with our demographic. They don't want to read too many things on a daily basis; they just want to read important things. We try to respect their time.

SM: I don't think people have time to read more than three or four pieces a day. OM: If we do four good pieces, I think that is really solid. Anything more than that is a stretch.

SM: Your total network traffic is approaching two million? OM: Close to it.

SM: And the vision of the company is to build a sort of mini Time Warner with a collection of Web sites? OM: I won't be that arrogant.

SM: Are you following what Time Warner is doing with companies like Adify? OM: I have not. There are several reasons for that; mainly I need to worry about my own thing. But I do know what they're doing, and what their model is about. I think it will be interesting to see what happens with them.

SM: What about other ad networks – are you seeing other innovations in the industry? OM: So far, to be honest, nothing has grabbed my attention. The game is still all about selling CPMs, which is what blogs are annoyed about. I think this is why I feel the guys at FM do a better job, because they're educating the market at the same time. They're selling sponsorships, and that yields much better revenue for blogs.

SM: Sponsorship is not a performance-based metric. OM: True, but I think that's the part of the business that needs attention from everybody. The whole industry needs to think in terms of how you're going to value these assets. That is very crucial.

SM: On the other end of the spectrum, I think Google is doing a very bad job of selling blog ads. Between Google at one end and FM at the other, there remains huge opportunity. OM: There is a massive opportunity – I agree with you. This whole business could use a bit more transparency. There are a lot of things you can't yet get on a daily basis. We can't even get decent stats.

SM: I agree, the whole analytics and monetization of the long tail side are big opportunities. That's one of the reasons I asked if you're tracking Adify because they're trying to fill that gap to some extent. Any other thoughts? OM: The only thought I had is that I wish I had more time to hang out with my friends, like you. Thank you for inviting me for the chat, it was fun. I feel like you're my therapist!

[Note: GigaOM switched from FM to IDG at the end of 2008. By then, GigaOM had amassed seven sites as part of the network.]

RAFAT ALI, PAIDCONTENT

Rafat Ali is a journalist, pioneering blogger, and entrepreneur.
Editor & Publisher *has called Rafat "journalism's poster boy for career independence from news companies." When faced with the repeated challenge of finding work, struggling and juggling the joys of job search and visa issues, Rafat eventually created his own.*

In the face of the deepening recession of 2009, I hope some will follow in his footsteps. I hope some will stop searching, and instead start creating.

SM: Where did you grow up, Rafat? RA: I was born in the UK, but my family is from the northern part of India. My father was a professor and lived in the US, the UK, and other parts of Europe. For the first five years of my life, I grew up in Denver. Then we moved back to India, where I lived until I was 25.

SM: What did you study? RA: I earned my engineering degree in computers in 1996, which was when the Internet had just started coming to India. We studied all of the underlying architectures of networks, and we knew all the theories. But we didn't have any life experience. I became disillusioned two years into the coursework and wanted to get into writing.

SM: Why disillusioned? RA: I felt I would have the same conventional thoughts as every other engineer and doctor, which is what it seemed everybody in India wanted to be. I thought copywriting would be interesting – that advertising was what I wanted to do with my life. It was a very glamorous lifestyle in India at that point.

I started reading everything about advertising. At the university library there were 50 books on advertising, and I read every single one of them. They were not new books; they were old classics. There was one trade magazine, *A&M* [*Advertising & Marketing*], and I would read that.

I finished school fine, and then I started applying to some advertising agencies and kind of got lost at that point. I was told I didn't have the experience, or that I could get a far better salary as an engineer. Entry-level copywriting is very bad in terms of salary. I finally got a job at a PR agency as an intern. I figured if I got an entry into PR I could make the jump to copywriting. I made 2,000 rupees [about $45] a month, which was not enough to live on in New Delhi. My family sent me some money each month, and that's how I survived.

Through PR work, I was exposed to a lot of journalists. I didn't like PR because I had to suck up to them. I figured I should try to become a journalist and write about the advertising industry. This was in 1997 and I applied to the editor of the industry's only trade magazine in India, *A&M*, which, of course, I'd been reading for years. The editor laughed at me because I wrote a long letter explaining how much I loved the magazine and the industry, and talking about everything I had been going through. He called me and told me I was crazy but he would hire me anyway. Unfortunately, the pay was worse than my internship.

I started at *A&M* by editing other people's copy. I recommend this to anyone who says they want to be a journalist. Starting by editing other people's copy is a great tool. I then began writing about the advertising industry, and my editor was really good. Soon the first India Internet World trade show arrived. The guy who wrote about technology for the magazine was out sick, and because my editor knew about my background in technology, he felt I would know something about this.

They hosted a convention for journalists to show off high-speed Internet. I went and saw graphic browsing, saw the Web, and met a lot of US experts who had been brought over for the conference. That's how I got the bug. I started writing about Internet advertising for *A&M*. But I realized there was only so much I could write about in India as we were simply following US trends. So, I decided to apply to five universities to obtain a master's in journalism, and was accepted to Indiana University. They had a new media fellowship, which I was fortunate enough to receive.

SM: The fellowship you received enabled you to attend Indiana University. Were there any requirements tied to that fellowship? RA: Two of us were given a fellowship, and our mandate was to create an intranet for the university's professors to use. It sounded grand, but we couldn't achieve it over the year and a half I was there because professors didn't want to collaborate. We gave that up; the school realized it was not going to happen. We were also teaching assistants for Web Writing 101 and for Web Design. It was basic back then; we started with Netscape Navigator. After the first semester we changed over to Dreamweaver.

Bloomington was near Chicago, so I subscribed to the *Chicago Tribune*, which published one of the first mainstream stories about blogging – Julia Heller wrote about what blogs were.

SM: What year was this? RA: It was 1999. I still have her story somewhere, although it's not online anymore. Salon.com did a story on blogs as well, and some of the early bloggers' names came up. Since I was teaching Web design to kids, I decided to start a blog documenting my journey as a student coming to America, learning a new culture. Coming from India to the middle of Indiana was tough. I had to adjust to an area that was completely white; there were 3% non-whites in the whole university. I didn't have any friends the first year. When I left India I did it with a mindset of rejecting everything. I wanted to move to a new country, start over. I now realize it wasn't the best thing. Studies were going great, but life outside of studies was horrible. That's what I documented on my blog.

SM: Were people reading it? RA: They were. It developed into this ironic look at American life from an outsider's perspective. I did it for a year and a half, and it gained a good following. I learned a lot about blogging, the blogging culture, and being part of that ecosystem. I finished my schooling in December 2000 with the maximum GPA possible in journalism.

SM: Were companies actively hiring journalism majors? RA: I came out at a really bad time. The Internet bubble had burst, and I wanted to write online. I was teaching, reading, studying, and writing Internet. I did get some interviews with consulting firms, and one job I almost took. I pretty much had no choice but to move to New York. I had one year left on my visa to work. My best friends in India had come to the US via the software route, and that's where they were living.

They were generous to let me stay with them for the first six months I was there. I got an internship at Inside.com, a news site covering all things media. They started in May of 2000, right after the bubble burst, and only lasted 18 months. I was there for eight of those months. It was a great ride. I started at $6 an hour, working three days a week. They were then bought by Brill Media Ventures. A lot of people got laid off, but I was below the threshold at $6 an hour, so they brought me along. Steve Brill then hired me as a journalist.

We were running out of money, and then September 11th hit. That was a huge blow, and we closed down in October. I was banking on them sponsoring me for an H1 [visa]. I had already moved to Manhattan, so I sent an e-mail to Jason Calacanis at *Silicon Alley Reporter*, who had been reading my stuff, and I got an interview.

> *I told them to hire me for two months, and if they didn't like my stuff, fire me. He hired me right there.*

SM: Did you pursue *Silicon Alley Reporter* for the magazine, or the Web site? RA: When I joined the magazine was shut down, so I wrote for the Web site. I did daily stories. This was in 2002, which is also when I started paidContent.org.

SM: paidContent was your own venture, right? RA: It was. After September 11th, blogging started becoming mainstream. I wrote about blogs a lot at Inside.com. A couple of my friends had started writing blogs and got their names around. I felt this was a way to get my name out there, because it seemed to me that *Silicon Alley Reporter's* Web site was going to be following their magazine. I felt that starting a blog would show what I covered as a journalist and what my area of expertise was.

I named it paidContent because at that point the bubble had burst. Internet advertising had fallen down. People felt you'd have to pay to access Web sites, so the trend was away from advertising models, toward paid subscription models. I registered the .org domain because the .com was already registered. I never expected it to get as big as it did. I had a few journalist friends, and it started growing by word of mouth.

By the end of 2002 I was sick of New York. PaidContent was still going, but that was the only thing I had going. I decided to move to London. I was a British citizen, even though I had never lived there. That decision was huge for me because when I moved to the US, I had intended to stay there for the rest of my life. But in

January of 2003 I moved to London. I didn't know anybody in London, although I had a few friends who were close to the city. One of my long-lost aunts from India had a big house in East London. Her family knew this was how people came over from India and Pakistan to London, so they were used to people coming to their house and staying for a few months.

I stayed with them for about four months while I hunted for a job. I kept updating paidContent while I was job hunting, which was good because I wasn't making very much headway finding work in London. Then I got a lucky lifeline where somebody from Germany thought I would make a good keynote speaker at a German-language Internet conference. They were actually willing to pay me €2,500 to go to a conference in Germany. I had never spoken publicly in my life, and here I was supposed to give a one-hour speech from behind a podium on paid content as a trend.

SM: Did you have any strategy associated with paidContent? RA: An interesting thing I had done from the start was to develop an e-mail newsletter. I copied all the blog posts of the day and sent them out via an e-mail newsletter. At that point RSS had just come into play.

The thing about e-mail newsletters, which is still true today, is that you have a viral presence in somebody's inbox day in and day out.

The value of that is huge. I didn't think this through then, but the value was definitely there.

SM: How many e-mail newsletter subscribers and Web site visitors did you have at that point? RA: This was in 2003 and it was probably a couple hundred. At that point I was still hoping to find a job in London as a journalist, but some offers to advertise on my site made me think twice. I was interviewing for just about any job possible. I interviewed for a job at a magazine where I would have been writing about mining. Thankfully, I did not get it.

I finally started responding to e-mails asking if I would take ads. Even though I was covering the ad industry, I didn't know much about running a business. I knew the industry, I wrote about the industry, and I knew the terminology, all of which helped, but I didn't know how to operate the business side. I wanted a monthly flat rate, and I was able to charge $400 a month for a banner on my site.

A US company was the first to advertise on the site. When other companies started seeing their competitors advertising on my site, they started contacting me as well, which is how advertising revenues started growing.

SM: And when did you start mocoNews? RA: I launched it about a year after paidContent, which puts it about mid-2003. I had seen what kids in London were doing with their phones. They had different dynamics in their interactions, and while I was covering the mobile space on paidContent, I realized it was a large enough space to need separate attention. I also launched a digital music site, which I killed a few months later. Initially, I thought online music was going to become this big trend.

SM: Were you writing for all of them? RA: I was doing it all. The majority was actually aggregation. I was putting it all together when nobody else was. This was after the bubble, and there were no media companies that wanted to touch this space. My site became the only place where anyone was covering the ad industry and viable business models in it.

By this time ads had started coming in, and I started getting more invitations to speak, including invitations to Boston and New York. That was bittersweet for me because when I left the US I was really angry at the whole American system. I swore I would never come back. But the first blogging business conference was in Boston in 2003. At that point you could see blogging as a business.

SM: You said you became known because you were the only one covering the ad space? RA: I became well known around 2003, when *WiredNews* did a story on me about blogging for bucks. I had started making $30,000 to $40,000 a year, so it was a business. I started *European Digital Media Weekly*, did a few issues of that, and then shut it down because I had decided to return to the US.

SM: What prompted the move back to the US? RA: I met my future wife when I was living in New York. She was going to NYU. We dated for a while, then she moved to San Francisco and I moved to London. After a year she came to visit an aunt of hers in London. We rekindled our relationship and decided to get married. I was earning a decent amount of money, and I could do it from anywhere. Initially, the idea was that she would move to London. The reality, however, is that I was covering a US market from London. And she was from Los Angeles, so we decided I'd move to Los Angeles. That was in March of 2004. We still had not gotten married, but we were engaged. We weren't living together because that's not allowed in our religion or culture, but I was in Los Angeles and she was in Orange County, so just an hour's drive from each other.

SM: How did getting married affect the business? RA: I had to go away for about 40 days because my wife, who is of Indian origin, was from South Africa. The marriage was in South Africa, and the reception was going to be in India. The entire ordeal was going to take 40 days. There was no way I would be able to run the site during that time. But I knew I couldn't stop the site; I had a responsibility to the readers as well as the advertisers who were paying me. I tried to hire two people for two months each – one to run mocoNews, and one to run paidContent. I posted a job listing on my site and got a lot of resumes. That's when I hired Staci

[Kramer] and James [Quintana Pearce]. While Staci didn't apply for the job, I already knew her. We had both worked at Inside.com. And James applied from Australia for the mocoNews position.

Both of them were virtual hires, just for the time I was gone. I had bought a new laptop which I figured I could take to India, log in, and check my e-mail. It was a Gateway laptop, so it was cheap. The first night the computer blew up because of the voltage fluctuations. There was no service center in India, and whatever money I had saved through the site had been put into the wedding. Then a week after I left, the servers on the hosting company melted. I was in the middle of getting married, traveling to India, with Staci and James covering part-time, and we now had to find another host. Luckily we had archives on our site.

When I came back I made some decisions. The economy was coming back, so advertising was paying more. I decided to ask those two to continue beyond the two months, and ultimately they came on full-time as contractors. Then in early 2005 I started getting interest from people who wanted to invest in us.

SM: What types of people were wanting to invest? RA: Industry-type people who were readers of the sites. They were senior executives who had recently left jobs, or angel investors who were reading the articles. I wasn't approaching them; they were approaching me. I knew nothing about getting investments. A group of five industry luminaries, all senior executives, were going to take a majority stake in my company for $100,000. Those were desperate times, and I didn't know any better. I hired a lawyer here through some references, which cost me about $25,000 because negotiations went back and forth. Then I got cold feet and went out, then came back in, and at the end of all of this he told me, "Rafat, forget that I'm a lawyer for a second. I'm telling you this as your friend: Do not take this deal." And I listened. It created a lot of ill will; I had known these guys for six months, and I walked away at the last minute.

SM: You turned down some private investors; what about institutional investors? RA: We started to get interest from companies who wanted to buy us in late 2005. I had a friend who had a friend who helped me sort through it, and we went through the normal gyrations. We had meetings with three companies, and at the end of the day I decided they were not looking at us as a company; they were only looking at us as talent to hire. I didn't see that as a good option.

> *It would have meant security, but I knew there was more potential if we did it on our own.*

We then decided to try and bring readers of the two sites together in an offline event, what I called the mixer. We had our first mixer in June 2005 in Los Angeles. I put a notice on the site to see what reaction I would get, and I got tons of response. I didn't have the resources to put it all together, so the readers helped. We got a venue because one of the readers knew somebody at the Viceroy Hotel. A couple of companies who were advertisers actually went ahead and sponsored the mixer. The first mixer had 350 people.

SM: What kind of sponsorships? RA: We earned about $12,000 total from three sponsors. We didn't have too many expenses because we got the venue at cost. That was our first event, which was proof of concept. I didn't know we were going to get into events that heavily.

SM: That brings us to 2006? RA: Yes. In January 2006 I got a call from Alan Patricof asking to know more about the company. I gave him a 20-minute rundown of what we were doing. I knew he was getting into the VC game again, and as he was speaking to companies in the space our site's name kept coming up. He had founded *New York Magazine* way back; he knew journalism. And I knew that if I was going to take money it had to come from somebody who knew the news media business.

I met Alan the next week in New York at a conference. Within 20 minutes of questions and answers, I knew he understood exactly what I was going through. I had a wife, two part-time people, and was tackling everything alone. He laid out the challenges of my business, which took me four years of experience to learn, better than I could have described them. At that point we decided we'd get the investment done, it would just take time. I didn't even have a balance sheet. He introduced me to a part-time CFO who literally came to my house, pulled all of the receipts, and put it all together.

Even though I had advertisers, I hadn't invoiced them for months on end. I would only invoice them when the money in my bank account was getting low, invoicing them for four to five months at a time.

> *I learned that when you start a company you need to spend money on keeping the books in order.*

Sorting out the finances delayed us six months.

SM: When did you finally close the investment deal with Alan Patricof? RA: It was in the middle of 2006. I believe it closed in June.

SM: How much was the investment? RA: We didn't announce the amount, but it was less than $1 million. We brought in a part-time COO whose main job was to pull this business out of my bedroom. He was working at some other company in Los Angeles and had an office already. I wasn't working out of his office, but it was good to have a part-time COO who had actual office space to work out of.

We started putting in HR policies. We officially made Staci and James employees and brought others on as well. We also hired a salesperson. This was all happening in 2006, which was a very rapid growth year for us.

SM: What kind of revenues did you hit in 2006? RA: We crossed $1 million in 2006.

SM: What was your split between advertising and events? RA: In 2006 we did four or five mixers. They were all low-cost and were getting sponsored. We did one in New York in July of 2006, which 700 people attended. That's when we literally landed on the face of New York media. Alan invited Arthur Salzberger, the head of the *New York Times*, to be the speaker. He accepted, which gave us strong editorial content at that mixer.

His digital people were reading us at that time, so I interviewed him about blogging and NewYorkTimes.com, and things of that nature. At that point in 2006, the split was still heavily online.

SM: Did your traffic and ad rates increase? RA: We've never sold by CPM, and still don't. We have flat-fee sponsorship.

SM: Do you have salespeople doing that for you? RA: We do now. We have four full-time employees in our sales department.

SM: In 2006 did you have your own salespeople? RA: I was still doing part of it, and we had one commission-only part-time sales person. It has always been our own; we never outsourced any part of it. My thought was that advertisers who understand the industry can only be sold to by somebody who is part of the company, who knows what we write about and how we're covering the industry. That was my rationale for not outsourcing.

Federated Media had not started at that point. John Battelle called before he started Federated and said, "Whatever you're doing,

I can do it." I literally remember his words. My response was, "Go ahead and do it. Why are you calling me?" I didn't exactly know what he was starting; I thought he was going to start a competitor to us. But he didn't. Instead he started Federated Media, which was a servicing company to these blogs.

I did realize that blog advertising models were coming online, and I did evaluate some, including theirs. Ultimately it was a sales service model that took 20–30% off the top. I couldn't see the point in outsourcing the advertising at that rate since I could do it organically with my sales force at the same rate.

SM: Who are your primary advertisers? RA: Over the years it's broadened quite a bit. The focus quickly expanded to cover all digital media. We follow all the ways content is paid for, whether it's subscription, hybrid models, pay per view, etc. Initially, the advertisers were software companies selling subscriptions to media companies. Over the years they've ranged from mobile content players to broadband and video companies. But as we started doing conferences, content companies got involved. Media companies had no reason to be involved until we started doing the conferences, then they wanted to be associated with the industry.

We also saw some advertising from digital media investment banks who were looking to do specialized deals. There were a few law firms. Even now we're not that strong in the area of law firms. That's one growth area we want to focus on.

SM: Segmentation is always good. Niche is good. RA: This is why in 2005 I started contentSutra, the India site. I started that site because I knew the market and it was English speaking on the business side. The thought was we would start a site at the time when foreign investors, media companies, VCs, and others were starting to enter India. We would help them navigate the Indian digital media market, both online and mobile.

A few months down the line our premise was proven completely wrong. The market wasn't ready. It became a site for the Indian digital media executives. That's still true now.

SM: Were you still having success with your conferences? RA: We did our second conference last year in New York on future business media. Some of the biggest names in the industry were there. Within two weeks of announcing the conference, News Corp. made a bid on Dow Jones, Thompson and Reuters merged, and Fox announced their business channel. All these big events in the business media industry happened within a few weeks of our announcing our Future of Business Media Conference. It was just the greatest timing for us. It was sold out, and we had great sponsors.

All of this was going on, and then late last year we started paidContent:UK to cover the UK market.

SM: Is it safe to say you were at a few hundred thousand page views per month across all of the sites by the end of last year? RA: Yes. We're over a million page views across our sites. We have about 50,000 newsletter subscribers and 40,000 RSS subscribers. One of the frustrations I have had is that people look at us as one blog. We are not. We are four different blogs, we have conferences, and we have newsletters. Most of the senior people in the industry read us through the newsletter. They actually have jobs, so they get it once a day in the morning, then they go do their jobs. They're not going to the site five times a day obsessively. This has been consistent over the six years of the site.

> *The phrase we hear is, "We wake up with you," and if you think about it, that's the most powerful thing you can dream of.*

A lot of people say they ditch the *Wall Street Journal* and the *New York Times* for the newsletter. One executive told me he reads the newsletter before he sees his wife's face in the morning. When I hear things like that, it really makes me understand the value of loyalty, and the power of being their daily read. There's a reason we send the newsletter at 6:00 a.m. EST.

SM: Can you talk about the recent sale of the company?
RA: We were in the middle of raising our second round. We decided somewhere, probably mid-2007, that we could leverage more money. For all intents and purposes we were still bootstrapped. If we could get a specific amount of money, we could hire another person; it was simple math. That's how we were growing. We were always resource-strapped.

Industry activity was reaching a fever pitch, and competition was coming in. When I started I was the only one doing this. Since then, everyone has raised their game. The *Wall Street Journal* started covering a lot of stuff, the *New York Times* started, and it just became a lot more competitive.

SM: It is a very low "barriers to entry" type of business.
RA: That is true. The first thing we decided was we needed to bring in a CEO. I knew we needed someone to drive the business. I was killing myself driving everything. That's what I wanted to grow out of; the company had to grow beyond me. So, we decided to raise a second round to enable us to hire a CEO and a chief sales officer.

It just so happened that it all occurred in reverse. Two candidates, a CEO and a chief sales officer, fell in our laps before we went on the fundraising round. We did that with the knowledge that having senior management in place would help us be more attractive to VCs and I wouldn't have to do this on my own.

Nathan Richardson came in, and he was literally the "dive-right-in" type on fundraising issues. The reality is he didn't do any of the CEO duties until we got bought by Guardian.

SM: Were you pitching to Guardian to raise money? RA: We were thinking about strategic investors or venture capital for raising money. We decided not to go the strategic route and instead took VC funding because we were concerned about conflict of interest – right of first refusal for exit, and all that stuff. It was just too complicated for a small company like us.

I had known the Guardian people very well for years. The first person who ever expressed interest in our being a part of Guardian was Simon Waldman. In 2003, when I was living in London, he mentioned that my site should be a Guardian property, and he was the head of Guardian's online properties at the time. I never thought about it seriously at that point.

We had some term sheets on the table, and the valuation was very competitive. Guardian came in, and a lot of things clicked immediately. Whoever was going to buy us had to leave us alone as a unit; that's what they wanted as well. From a journalistic perspective, we wanted to be part of a company that was upholding the values of journalism that we upheld. They're known for that, and they're digitally savvy – one of the most progressive firms in terms of what they do online. They also had good international outlets, and the nature of the sites we'd built gave us an international view. Even in terms of events, we'd done them in London and Barcelona. Whoever was going to buy us had to have that ethos, and Guardian has it.

SM: How does this fit with Guardian's growth plans? RA: They're entering India, and they're entering the US, which is one of the reasons they bought us. They believed in our growth plans. The growth plans that we were going to raise funding on are the same ones that Guardian bought us for. We have specific plans on scaling from here.

SM: How do you define "here"? What are the benchmarks in terms of revenues, visits, and other metrics? RA: We've doubled our revenues every year. We've grown from 2 to 30 people. We have offices in Santa Monica, New York, and London. We're now exploring potential allied verticals. We would like to add more verticals, which we can either start ourselves or potentially acquire from smaller properties. We've started on research reports, and we're going to launch an online advertising report that we hope will sell well.

We're starting to look at the data side of the business. We have a lot of archives and rich data from the past six years, all of which are very unstructured beyond a blog structure. If we want to know about certain deals in a certain sector in a particular value range, then we're out of luck, at least right now. We're going to try and build a robust database which offers potential revenues through a subscription service.

SM: So you're going to consider information services as well? RA: Yes. Information database services, which is a typical trade media mentality. We have no intentions of being a consumer company.

> *The key, I've always said, is we are the filter for an industry in chaos.*

For busy senior executives in this space, how do we organize it? First you organize based on the efficiency of consumption. We do that through blog posts and aggregation. At a conference, how do you pack in the most in a day or half a day? Even in research reports, how do readers get a snapshot of the market in a way that is most efficient to them? That's why we go into SEC filings, earnings reports, earnings calls, etc. We're trying to extract everything that is newsworthy. That's why we're not heavy on opinion. The goal is news, data, and context. Another great thing about Guardian is that they bought us with trust. They look at businesses on a long-term horizon.

SM: I think that is especially important, as it sounds like this is what you want to do with your life. Finding the right partner who will let you do that is important. RA: I've known a lot of individuals at Guardian. I watched the entry attempts in the US market. They tried to enter the US market via the consumer route by launching a weekly, and it didn't work. They realized the consumer route is not the way to enter, business-to-business is.

SM: Congratulations. This has been a great story, and I think you are very fortunate to have made the deal with Guardian before the market enters an extremely difficult phase.

J. R. Johnson, VirtualTourist

If you think only engineers start companies, think again. You've met journalists Om Malik and Rafat Ali, both great entrepreneurs. Now meet J. R. Johnson, a lawyer by training, but quickly becoming a serial entrepreneur.

To make the leap Johnson raised money – a very small amount – from friends and family. His mother kept the books, and while he and his two partners slogged away in a tiny apartment, she brought them food once a week, from Costco.

On life as a bootstrapper: "We had a Coffee Bean down the street," Johnson says, "and they had a punch card program: if you purchased 12 coffees you got another one free. These things were like gold to us. The Coffee Bean was our one indulgence. We would go buy the cheapest coffee they had, load it up with sugar and milk, and sit there and have our coffee. When we got the twelfth punch we'd order the extra large, ice blended coffee with an extra shot of espresso. It was a $6–$7 drink by the time we were done with it.

"My partner Tilman had a card with 12 punches, and he left it in his pants in the wash. He was so bummed he sat there and took these little pieces of paper, pieced them together, then

took Scotch tape and taped it all together so it looked like a laminated card. That's how desperate we were."

Startups require such frugality. A balanced, cushy life is not exactly what you sign up for when choosing to become an entrepreneur. There are significant trade-offs, but thankfully they can, as in Johnson's case, pay off handsomely.

SM: Let's start by going back to the beginning. Where does your journey start? JJ: I was born in Manhattan Beach, California, but raised in Westlake Village, a middle-class suburb on the Ventura County/LA County border. After high school I went to USC, where I studied business with an emphasis on entrepreneurship. After USC I took a year off before going to law school.

SM: Why did you study entrepreneurship? Was there a history of entrepreneurship in your family, or was it just something that captured your imagination? JJ: I've always been interested in entrepreneurship. When I was a little kid I was always doing different things. In fourth grade I found a Styrofoam airplane supplier. I rode my bike down to his factory, not too far from my house. I bought a bunch of them, took them to school, and sold them for $0.50 an airplane. Entrepreneurship has always been in me, but not my family. My dad was a lawyer.

SM: You went to law school after USC – was that to follow in the footsteps of your father? JJ: It was. My grandfather was a lawyer, and my dad is a lawyer, so it was predetermined for me. I went on to law school knowing it was a great education and a nice safety net – you can always get a job as a lawyer – even though I knew in my heart I would be starting businesses.

SM: What year did you graduate? JJ: I graduated from USC in 1993 and from law school in 1997. I did law school at SMU, in Dallas, so I came back to California and took the bar here.

SM: You came back to California in time for the Internet to take off. JJ: It was getting started. I wasn't completely into it yet, but it was something I was reading about and seeing these cool things happening. I was working for a law firm, and they sent me to Germany in early 1999 to speak at a conference of startup companies. There were a couple hundred people in the main hall of a brewery, and I gave a talk on going public and raising money in the US so these German entrepreneurs could have an idea how things were done here. Afterwards, these guys came up to me and told me about vTourist.com, a Web site they had.

We hit it off pretty well. They were students at a great university; I had traveled a bit in college. In the spring of 1991 I did a semester at sea, where I went around the world. That was my first real exposure to world travel. I was thinking back on that experience as I talked to these guys, and one experience I had in India really popped out. The ship pulled into Madras [now Chennai], and we were scheduled to go up to see the Taj Mahal. We were only there for a week and didn't have a lot of time. The first night we ran into this traveler from New Zealand who'd been drinking, and he would not stop talking about Darjeeling and how it's the greatest place in the world. We thought it sounded great, so me and my buddy scrapped our trip to the Taj Mahal and went to Darjeeling. It was really the coolest experience. To this day it's my fondest travel memory hands down, and it came about because of a random, chance meeting with a stranger. That's how we came up with this idea of building a user-generated content platform to enable others to share their travel experiences.

SM: When did you launch VirtualTourist.com? JJ: In 1999 I started talking to Tilman Reissfelder, who's now my partner. He had the Web site, which at the time had a clickable map, some open source content, and some paid links. Reflecting back on my travel experiences, I suggested we build something that gave people a platform to share their travel-related experiences, ideas, and desires. At the time the only community sites were GeoCities,

Tripod, and others like those. It was unorganized user-generated content. We didn't want to do that. We wanted it organized so it could be useful to third parties when they were planning a trip.

We put together 13 different categories that we felt would be useful to travelers. We modeled it after the travel guidebooks at the time, launching the site on January 3, 2000.

On the business side of things, before I quit my job at the law firm one of my partners invested $50,000. Then we raised a friends and family round of $263,000 in November of 1999. That's the only money the business ever raised.

SM: When you raised a friends and family round, who was willing to bet on you? JJ: My parents didn't have any money. My grandfather put a little bit in. We raised it from 17 different people. There was a girl from high school, a friend from Westlake – it was literally a hodgepodge of people who put money in.

SM: It often is. So your total startup capital was $313,000? JJ: That was it. It was my strategy at the time, because I'd talked to a few people and come to the conclusion that people didn't understand user-generated content. A common response I got was, "Why would somebody want to read what somebody else has written? Isn't that what we have professional journalists and authors for?" I decided to launch the site in January, let it run for three months, and then take some of the user-generated content to raise a large, professional VC round. I set up a bunch of appointments for April of 2000. But it just so happens that in March of 2000 the Internet bubble burst and everything started falling apart. Not only were people not investing in Internet companies, they were also avoiding investments in Internet content companies. Nobody would touch us with a 10-foot pole.

We had a little office in Santa Monica. We had hired nine people, investment banker buddies and lawyer friends, to come on board and build out our team to go raise money. I had to tell my friends to go back to their real jobs, and we moved out of our tiny office and into an apartment. I was kicking myself for a long time for not taking $2 to $3 million earlier, which we could have done, but we wanted the higher valuation.

Giampiero Ambrosi, who is still the general manager, moved into Tilman's apartment. From then on it was just the three of us, plus my mother who helped out by doing the books. It was very depressing. My mom brought food from Costco once a week while we tried to figure out what to do with this Web site we'd built.

SM: What was your plan for monetizing the site? How did you do it? JJ: During that time I convinced GoTo.com, which later became Overture.com, to allow us to take their paid links and put them into our content. I made the argument that a user who had to click six times to get down to our London page was a better advertising target than someone typing in "London hotels."

The irony of it all is how successful Google has been and how GoTo fell flat because they wouldn't let people take their paid links and put them into content. I finally convinced them to do that, and we started making a little money. Advertisers started coming back in late 2001. In 2002 we actually started making enough money to pay ourselves.

SM: How much traffic did you have when you started making money? JJ: I don't even remember what the number was. The site always had decent traffic because it was a very old URL. That was something that Google weighed very heavily in their algorithm in the early days.

SM: You got organic traffic because of the URL name? JJ: Yes. As soon as we started putting in user-generated content, we picked up even more SEO, which brought in more members who contributed more, thus helping our SEO even further. This was a real positive snowball.

> *We always knew that in the worst-case scenario we could go into cockroach mode and just hide out in the dark for a while and let the content grow.*

The more content we had, the more people we would get and the more valuable the company would become. The one thing we did right was pick the correct business model, a model that was able to sustain itself on very little investment. As long as we kept the server plugged in, it was able to grow.

SM: How did you sell ads? Did you have your own ad sales force? JJ: We didn't have our own sales force until late 2002. It was some small network stuff and a lot of Overture links. When Google came on, we swapped them out. Early on we only got a very small percentage of the revenue share, but now it has swung completely in the opposite direction. What we were giving GoTo at the time is what we're getting from Google now. Having another player in the space has been very favorable to publishers.

SM: In terms of AdSense, they don't share a great deal with publishers. I can't imagine it could have been that much worse with Overture. JJ: We didn't have a ton of traffic when we made the switch, but for us it was more money than what we had been making. I don't recall the numbers off the top of my head, but it was enough to get a real office and start getting some salary.

SM: You must have had millions of visitors to do that, right? JJ: I think we were right at one million unique visitors a month at the time.

SM: What type of traffic levels are you currently seeing? JJ: We're seeing five to six million unique visitors a month.

SM: What happened after 2003, when you got your base business going? JJ: We started hiring more people as needed. It's now a complete cash flow business. The more money we make, the more people we're able to hire. We started doing some ad sales in-house, so we hired a couple guys to run that. Since we had inventory that could be sold, those employees paid for themselves.

Then we started looking around at different opportunities in the space. One thing our advertisers wanted was more conversions, and our users were still looking for a better way to book and compare rates. We came up with the concept for OneTime.com, a booking comparison site that we launched in April 2004 as a separate company.

We've always been focused on content. We wanted the best content, and only the best content, on VirtualTourist. We did not want booking clutter competing in the space. There are a lot of subtleties that go into user-generated content. The content contributed on Orbitz, Expedia, or Travelocity is very different from our content.

SM: In 2004 you launched this comparison shopping site, OneTime. What was significant about 2003 that made you do that? JJ: I don't know if there was anything really monumental; we were just trying to focus on growing the business. We were very focused on finding ways to monetize all of our content, and figure out how to put ads on the pages without destroying the user experience.

SM: How did the ad monetization change as you went from pure AdSense to your own ad sales force? JJ: It was nothing overnight; it was pretty slow. We always had enough inventory and had never completely sold it out until the end of 2007. Before that we had plenty of inventory, so we were able to plug in whatever we sold, and we ran it that way.

SM: Who were the advertisers you were able to tap into?
JJ: American Express was our biggest advertiser; they were with us three to four years nonstop. The travel guides were also pretty big. The airlines, hotels, and online travel agents were other big advertisers. That was really our focus.

SM: What shape did the business take in 2006 and 2007?
JJ: On the ad side of the business, we went after convention visitor bureaus. They spent a lot of money in TV, newspapers, and magazines but were really slow to get online. We really tapped into them, and it was a perfect fit. We had a bunch of people on the site who were trying to travel, and a bunch of the CVBs who were trying to entice travelers to come to their city or country. That was a big boost in our advertising sales model.

In 2006, it became fun. This was where we always wanted to be. We were starting to make some money and do some of the things we always wanted to do. We were able to offer users the ability to save reviews into their own guidebooks and print out their own custom travel guides. We were able to do things we were never able to do before. Going from a negative cash flow to a positive cash flow really helps morale.

SM: You had to be cash flow positive for the majority of your business, correct? When did you start breaking even?
JJ: It's easy to break even when you're not paying yourself anything. It wasn't a typical scenario where we had a million dollars, ran with negative cash flow for a while, and eventually turned the corner. This was something that was positive cash flow on a monthly basis.

> *SM: Exactly. You only had $313,000, so after that you had to be cash flow positive. JJ: We spent that very early on in 2000, and when it was gone we decided we could quit or believe in what we were doing and move into an apartment. We put everything else in our lives on hold while we got it going. It was part stubbornness, part stupidity, and part faith that what we were doing was going to work at some point.*

It really comes down to a few iterations of the same message. We were just too stubborn to let it go. When you're desperate you get creative. None of it is rocket science. People are doing it to monetize their sites everywhere now. But back in 2001 and 2002 what we did was unique.

SM: How many people did you have when you sold the company? JJ: We had 35 people.

SM: Can you break them down functionally? JJ: There were 35 across both companies – 15 people on OneTime and 20 on VirtualTourist. Half of them were tech people or developers, and the next largest group would be sales. After that would be the managers and executives. We had a general manager for both One-Time and VirtualTourist, as well as a CFO, and a VP of sales on VirtualTourist who had seven people working for him in various capacities. That was a four-person sales team with a support staff, covering the entire country.

> *SM: Without venture capital, did you find it difficult to recruit people? JJ: We couldn't get a big resume from Yahoo! to come over.*

But on the sales side, we were just hoping for people who had some sales experience. We were really looking for people who had a willingness to learn and work hard. We taught quite a few people the entire business.

The perfect example of this is the general manager of OneTime, Dena Yahya. She was our fifth or sixth employee; I think she started in 2003. We gave her a business development title, but she really came in just to help me with various tasks running the business. She learned the business, search engine marketing, and search engine optimization, and she now runs OneTime. When we sold the business, OneTime accounted for 50% of revenue.

It was tough to recruit, and it still is. It is a little easier now that we're a part of Expedia – I guess it gives people more confidence. When it's just a few of you, getting good people is tough. For whatever reason we were able to get good, smart people who may not have had all the experience, but who wanted to learn, who were smart, and who did a great job.

SM: When you hired people, did they have equity in the company? JJ: Yes, that was one way to entice people to join us.

SM: What was the revenue level when you sold the company, and how did the sale take place? Did you start shopping the company, or did buyers come to you? JJ: We were constantly approached by a number of different people. We just never wanted to sell the business. VirtualTourist was number two after TripAdvisor when it came to user-generated content. It was big. We were doing five to six million unique users a month. We never did any PR, so we weren't well known outside of the space, but within the space everybody knew us.

When we finally decided we wanted to sell, I interviewed some investment bankers. I ended up hiring a group out of San Francisco called Union Square Advisors, which is a new startup investment bank. They knew the space really well. And I really liked them; we just hit it off. From there we talked to everyone on the street, shopping the company. We gave 15 different presentations, and the best fit the whole way around was Expedia, so that's who we chose.

SM: Can you give me a bit of comparison with TripAdvisor? What year did they come about, and how did you feel about TripAdvisor versus your business? JJ: They started after us, actually, but I believe they launched in late 2000. They had some VC money, and they focused on hotels. It was a smart focus because hotels are obviously the largest ticket item people spend money on when traveling. It's obviously easier to monetize that traffic. They've now become a hotel buying guide.

SM: It sounds like that's where you ended up. They obviously understood your business. JJ: We always saw them as a competitor, so it was a little odd, but that's the nice thing about going through that process and talking to everybody out there. I wanted to make sure I was putting the company in the hands of someone who was going to take care of it and grow it. They knew how to grow this type of business, and they're already doing it. It really makes me happy knowing the VirtualTourist team is still working for VirtualTourist, which includes my mom and my brother. They're now working it under Expedia. Dena is still the GM at OneTime. They're not laying anyone off; they're hiring even more people. It's been a really good acquisition to date.

SM: What about you, are you still involved? JJ: I am not. That was part of the deal. When we started the company we all thought we were going to run it for 20 or 30 years. It was cash flow positive and we had a lot of fun. It was at the end of 2007, when I really wanted to focus on my next venture but couldn't get my head out of VirtualTourist, that we decided it would be best to just sell. That would enable me to focus on my next venture.

SM: So you intentionally negotiated yourself out of the deal? JJ: We had the team in place to run the day-to-day, so the business was in good enough shape that I felt comfortable doing that.

SM: What happens next? JJ: I've already invested a few million dollars into my next venture, where I have 18 people on the team. It's called Lunch.com. We're currently building it, and at some point I may take in some VC funding. We had a nice run last time and were able to avoid it on the first deal that we did. But I'm not sure if I'll deal with professional money guys going forward or not. I might start talking to some guys in the next six months or so. It is nice to have the financial ability to hire a great team and pay them what they deserve.

Six weeks out and I'm already knee-deep into the next venture – without a vacation!

SM: Is Lunch.com still stealth? JJ: There's a splash page where you can sign up for an invite. Right now it's a private invite. It won't be ready for a full launch for a couple months.

SM: Well, this has been a great story. I look forward to sitting down again for Lunch(.com).

GUILLAUME COHEN, VEODIA

Over the years, I have heard countless creative bootstrapping stories, but Guillaume Cohen's early years, boarding with future in-laws to save launch money, display a remarkable and rare pragmatism. (To say nothing of the pure generosity of his in-laws.)

Guillaume articulates one of the cardinal rules of bootstrapping: be careful whom you hire at the beginning. I've personally come to the same conclusion as Guillaume that early on, hiring senior executives is a waste of money. You need hands-on, roll-up-your-sleeves doers, even freelancers off eLance, to get the task at hand done.

SM: Where do you come from, Guillaume? What's your background? GC: I was born in Bordeaux, France. I grew up in the southwest of France, where my family still lives. I moved to Paris to study and lived there for about 10 years before moving to the States.

SM: You did all of your engineering schooling in Paris? GC: Yes. I went to the Ecole Polytechnique and ENSTA [Ecole Nationale Supérieure de Techniques Avancées], both in Paris.

SM: Did you work in France? GC: Very briefly. As I was finishing my degree, I worked in some startups part-time. Internships are required as part of the curriculum in France. I did that, but right after I graduated I came straight to the US.

SM: Why did you want to come to the US? GC: To be honest, I had friends here already, telling me that the surfing, quality of life, and weather were great in California. Obviously, being in high-tech, this is where things happen. That made sense. I first applied to do a master's here instead of at ENSTA in France. But I didn't get any scholarships, so I would've had to borrow money, so I decided to finish my studies in France, then get a job here.

SM: Where did you get a job? GC: I got a job at a company called Envivio. It was a spin-off of France Telecom in the video space. It was started by an alumnus of Polytechnique, which is how I got in touch. I joined them in March of 2001.

SM: What was the capacity of your employment with them? GC: I started first as a professional services engineer. I got involved with some big projects with clients like Citigroup. I understood the technology, and because I was in constant contact with the clients, I understood their needs as well. I started packaging the technology for a particular client, and it became a product that we started selling to more clients. Almost accidentally I created the enterprise market for Envivio, which initially was focused on the telecoms, selling them video equipment for IPTV. We basically started building this product for Citigroup, and this market grew out of it, which ended up being the majority of our revenue source.

SM: What was the enterprise product? GC: It was broadcasting for internal communications. Citigroup had analysts doing morning calls, briefing the brokers in the different branches. Typically they do a conference call, but they needed to broadcast in order to share not just audio but also video and recorded sessions as knowledge assets that could potentially be resold. It was really more IP television addressing enterprise scenarios.

SM: How big did Envivio become, and what was your evolution with them? GC: I stayed with them for five years. They now have 120 employees; when I joined there were 15. At some point they were involved in too many markets and they had to focus. The investors had invested more for the telecom market versus the enterprise, and Envivio decided to focus more on the enterprise, as well as on the broadcaster and telecom markets.

At the time I saw it, I realized I couldn't continue to grow that market because most of the profits from my business unit were funding the other units. I couldn't scale it or explore better business models because that would take me too far from the core strategy, so I decided to leave and start my own company and address what I'd heard and seen from my own customers about their needs and problems.

SM: Is that when you started Veodia? GC: Yes. I started it two and a half years ago.

SM: Did you just quit one day and start? How did you fund it? GC: First I had to work on my personal cost structure so I could leave my job and go without a salary. Fortunately, my future in-laws lived in Palo Alto, so I moved in with them before even getting married. They were great and provided me with a room I could use for work. I would bring engineers to the house and use the living room for seminars, and they would provide food as well.

I lived with them for a year and a half, and found a Stanford engineer, working for NASA, who helped me build the first prototype.

> *SM: How did you find him? GC: I sent an e-mail to the Stanford mailing list. We knew people in common, and he responded. We got involved and built this prototype, which helped us raise money from one angel.*

SM: What was the prototype? GC: It was almost a fully working product. It was a Web-based service that allowed a user to sign up for an account. It was a hosted, software-as-a-service model. It allowed you to broadcast live video from your browser, as long as you had a camera connected to the computer, and stream it live to thousands of people. You could also record it, manage your library of content, and share it via multiple devices. Obviously we took a lot of shortcuts because it was a prototype.

SM: How long did it take to build? GC: About six months.

SM: And you used the prototype to get angel funding? Who was the angel? GC: The angel was an individual I knew as a friend. I was able to raise $200,000. He liked me and what I showed him, but I didn't have to articulate a full business plan. It was based on faith in me and what he saw. That obviously helped; it allowed us to basically file some patents and pay for the lawyers to file those patents. We were also able to get a real office, even though it was small. We also hired a couple people on very small salaries, and we started to monetize the prototype.

That allowed us to sign a deal with Cisco WebEx. They selected us to be part of their WebEx Connect platform as their provider of video. It was a new product to a great customer base, but we also got new customers such as universities based on the reputation.

SM: How were you selling? GC: It was direct selling. People were finding us via the Web site. We had a free trial. People could start using it, then call us for an upgrade, a freemium SaaS model.

That model allowed us to extend the angel round, and we were able to raise another $1 million from another angel group. At the time we were talking to Genentech, who was very interested in our product. The guy from Genentech talked to a friend of his over the weekend. And this friend said he heard good things and asked about our financing situation, then pulled together a group of people to invest in our angel round.

I was also investing in PR. I hired a PR person very early on to create some buzz. That also really helps get traction with investors.

SM: Did you have any VCs talking to you, or just the angels?

GC: *At the time I took the money from the angels, I had some offers from VCs. We ended up going with the angels as it allowed us to build more value and wait to raise VC money under better terms. Angels were ready to go with a convertible note.*

SM: You raised the $1.2 million on a convertible note?
GC: Yes. We gave them a warrant with a discount on the Series A.

SM: Who was advising you on the mechanics of convertible notes and such? GC: I did everything myself. I read about them on blogs, and I learned about them from my lawyers as well.

SM: OK, so you had financing, a prototype product, and a WebEx partnership. What happened next? GC: We closed the $1.2 million in February of 2007, and from there started getting more clients and gaining more traction. We were written up in the *Financial Times*. Our user base grew, and I spent a lot of time with VCs looking at a real Series A round. We closed that round in November of 2007.

SM: How many customers did you have at that point? GC: We had a few dozen. They were enterprise customers like APC, and a few smaller ones. At the time we had a wide range of use cases. We built the service and threw it out there to see how people would use it, learning the use cases and where the real market opportunities were. We learned there were an infinite number of ways the product was used. Churches used it to broadcast their sermons; companies used it for product managers to create training videos; and individual bloggers used it to blog. People used it to broadcast events of their life.

> *We realized that to be a leader in the market we had to look at all of the use cases and identify the market opportunities.*

We studied the segmenting and, gathering the intelligence we had, correlated it with research. We had to make a decision of whether to focus on one use case or to become an enabler of all those use cases and work with partners to build the whole product.

SM: What did you decide? GC: We decided to become more of a platform. The potential of the core technology we'd built could be delivered in so many different ways. We re-engineered the product to make it more of a platform that empowers other products for specific use cases. If you want to use video as part of your sales process, we can enable that.

SM: Can you give me an example of an application Veodia is supporting? GC: We built a plug-in for Clearspace that allows you to record a video from within Clearspace. Any employee can create a video and share it internally with other employees, as well as share and receive videos from clients. It makes video a casual part of all business communications. We call ourselves an "agile video platform that empowers people to use video as part of their daily communications."

SM: To do that you need partnerships with the people who are going to do the actual applications. GC: Absolutely. Obviously the first one was with WebEx, and the most recent was with Jive Software. We have more in the works.

SM: How much of this thinking and decision making was done when you raised your VC round? GC: Not that much. We were honest with them up front and told them what use cases we had identified. We told them we were in the process of working through and categorizing them. What was important for the investors was seeing the huge potential in the technology and seeing all of the different use cases it could be applied to. They had faith that we could figure it out, and we understood what the important things were in evaluating the markets. We chose to focus on the right things first.

SM: How much did you raise in the VC round? GC: With the note it totaled up to an $8.3 million Series A.

SM: Who were the VCs? GC: It was Clearstone Ventures. They backed PayPal and a bunch of other great companies. We also had D. E. Shaw, which also has a venture capital group.

SM: There is more of that going on now. Hedge funds are increasingly getting involved in venture. How did they find you? GC: It was a personal connection; I knew someone there. They have a large fund set aside for VC, and they've hired partners from existing VC groups in the Valley.

SM: Was there a difference between your dealings with Clearstone, a traditional firm, and your dealings with D. E. Shaw? GC: D. E. Shaw has slightly more compliance requirements in terms of financial reporting. In terms of negotiating term sheets, it was not much different.

SM: In November of 2007 you raised the financing round – what happened next? GC: The reason we raised that money was to build the engineering team. We did that and invested more in the core technology. We did the re-engineering necessary to support our core strategy of being a platform.

SM: Is that re-engineering done? GC: Yes.

SM: Are people using it? GC: Yes. Sun Microsystems is going to deploy us as part of their internal learning system. They're going to enable all of their employees with the ability to create videos. They're going to harvest and capture every bit of knowledge their employees have in video, then share it with other employees, and potentially an external audience as well. That's part of the movement hitting the enterprise 2.0/3.0 area. Communication is changing internally and externally. We're very much a part of that movement. We bring the human aspect to it. And we do it in a way that's easy and can be used by any employee.

We also do it in a way that's compatible with enterprise requirements, which is important. Our platform is for the enterprise, which is not the case for most consumer services you find. Enterprises want things like the ability to integrate with their existing infrastructure, single sign-on, APIs, and security as well as some level of control. And they want very high visual quality. YouTube quality is not acceptable for an enterprise, even in casual use. If your COO wants to use it, he wants to look good.

SM: What else should we touch on in your story? GC: We now have 17 employees. We moved to a new office. We used to be in a basement in Palo Alto, and now we're in San Mateo.

SM: How much of an executive team do you have? GC: I was able to put a very strong team together. My VP of products comes from SAP, which is very core enterprise. He also works with the user experience group.

SM: How did you find him? GC: I met him at Office 2.0 in 2007. He became a friend, and at some point I approached him looking for recommendations for the position. Turns out he was interested. He was a startup guy working for a big company – happy, but a startup environment is more natural for him.

Our VP of engineering is the inventor of Rhapsody. He's a French guy also. He was a friend of a friend. He has been in the Valley longer than me.

A lot of the people I brought into the team were through personal connections. One of the people who started VideoLAN VLC, the open source project that's very successful and has been used in commercial projects, has joined us as well. I posted something on the VideoLAN mailing list for a consulting project. He replied, and when I was traveling in Europe I interviewed him in the Munich airport. He was doing an internship in Germany at the time. I was coming back from a trip, so I was dressed very casually. He was there with a suit and tie. I ended up hiring him and brought him over on a visa.

SM: How do you charge? What is your pricing model? GC: It's a SaaS model, which has two components. One is based on seats, depending on how many people you enable in your organization and how many people have a login on your existing platform. We can charge on a monthly, quarterly, or annual basis. You can start small, and if you like the technology, you can then buy more seats. It's low-risk, a WebEx model. Prove the technology, then start spreading.

By the time IT gets involved, it's too late to go back. And they embrace the technology because we make their lives easier.

SM: There is some revenue already in the company, right? GC: There's good revenue for a startup at our stage. In two and a half years we've gotten clients like Sun Microsystems that we can reference and are rolling out company wide. We also have recurring revenue, which is great. There's also a usage component: if a certain percentage of usage is exceeded, then we start charging based on bandwidth. It scales with usage.

SM: The online storage and bandwidth is on your infrastructure? GC: Yes, everything is completely cloud-based.

SM: Where do you go from here? GC: We've been investing a lot in building the teams. It has taken us more time to grow than we initially planned, which is not unusual.

SM: Do you have a head of sales? GC: No. We're now focusing on hiring product marketing people, trying to make sure we're not driven by technology, but rather by the market. We also just hired a marketing communication person to generate more awareness and leads. The next phase is to grow the business and sales.

> *For now, most of the sales are done by myself and another guy, who is in charge of client services. We didn't want to invest in a sales force until we had the formula figured out.*

Timing is everything. I am trying to optimize things and make sure we put money where we need to at the right time. I don't want to be too early for the market.

SM: That's smart. Sales scales well once you know what you are selling, to whom, and how. How long will your current money last you? GC: That depends on how quickly we grow the revenue. At least a year and a half. We raised a big round. We want to get as much value out of that as possible. We want to really grow revenue.

SM: What I really like is that you haven't gone and hired a lot of salespeople. Until you figure out repeatability in the sales cycle, there isn't much use hiring sales managers. GC:

They aren't going to define the product for you. Obviously, with the success we've had, we've been able to narrow the plans and align the product with our strategic goals. We know to whom we need to market.

SM: Can you talk about how the Sun Microsystems deal happened? Do you know how you penetrated that account? GC: In most cases it's people from the business groups who hear about us. In that case, the guy who found us is the CTO of learning services at Sun. He wants to find solutions to improve learning, and that's usually the best way for us to get the product up and running. That's generally the best way for us to target someone, because the business users are the people who best see the value. With other organizations we get approached by IT. But that's a cultural thing; some companies have IT groups that are forward thinking. However, if there's not a business group sponsoring the project, it's not going to happen. IT generally focuses on protecting themselves. That's why we think the best approach is through the business groups, and the later IT is involved, the better.

SM: Beyond IT, what you're saying is that training and learning organizations are great places to scale your account. That's where you would send your sales organization. GC: More and more companies now have someone in charge of collaboration. There are people in charge of improving communication with those new technologies. Technology people in those business groups are the ideal ones to target. They appreciate all the hooks the software has, and they see how we fit into their environment along with the benefit we bring to their business group. They are then advocates when the IT group is brought in, and they can directly counter any worries IT has. They're also advocates within the business group, and they can really envision how we'll help their group accomplish its role. They're the perfect individuals to target.

SM: How has your role as CEO evolved? GC: Each stage has been different. When there were just two of us, I was involved in building the prototype.

> *One of the big learning experiences for me, as a first-time CEO, is bringing in smart people who are much better than I am in their fields, then staying out of their way.*

I need to show them direction and vision, but leave them as much room as possible to realize their full creative potential. That works really well. Perhaps in the beginning I was too involved, but some of that was out of necessity. Having the money available to us now has enabled me to change my role, and I think I have learned and grown with the roles I have taken on.

What I am working really hard on now is the culture. I'm creating a culture where people feel proud and comfortable communicating. There's a book called *Leadership and Self-Deception* that I've made part of the new employee package. It focuses on communication and how people tend to behave in a way where they see themselves as victims, and as such they behave in a way that emphasizes the same behavior. They call it "being in the box." That applies not only to the work environment but also to personal life. It sounds basic, but I think it has helped me explain what I'm trying to build to my employees. They understand what I'm saying when I talk about openness and transparency.

SM: Those are good values. GC: They seem like obvious things, but they're difficult to achieve in organizations. Politics can happen very early, so I want to ensure that I establish the right culture very early. I think that whatever the culture is that I establish at this stage is important because I expect it to grow with the company. When there are 100 or 200 employees, I believe we'll have the same culture as long as I focus on it now.

SM: Thank you for sharing your story. Excellent bootstrapping!

WAYNE KROUSE, HYDRO GREEN ENERGY

Wayne Krouse was halfway through Ayn Rand's Atlas Shrugged *in 2001, when he was fired from his job at Exxon for creating trouble. The troublemaking had come in trying to do a buyout of a piece of his employer's business. Even when the deal fell through, the company anticipated more trouble. "I don't apologize for being a troublemaker," he laughs, recollecting how he was told to pack up one day. "I like to push people. I'm not a comfort zone kind of guy."*

Isolated but undeterred, Wayne survived four years on savings and 401(k) money, awaiting a patent he alone believed in. "It will never work," his uncle said. "Complete waste of time." But inspired by the character of Hank Rearden from Atlas Shrugged, *Wayne kept on until the pieces started falling into place.*

SM: Wayne, where do you come from? WK: I'm originally from Natchez, Mississippi. My family moved around a lot. We also lived in Houston and Memphis for periods of time, but we always came back to Mississippi. My senior year of high school we were in Memphis. I then went to Tulane University and got a degree in chemical engineering.

SM: Was there much of an entrepreneurial background in your family? WK: There is some on both sides of the family. On my mom's side my great-grandfather emigrated from Europe to Canada. My grandfather was born in Montreal, and they then moved to New York City and on to Helena, Arkansas. They eventually got to Natchez, where there was a lot of cotton and agricultural trade along the river. They came down and tried to buy and re-sell anything they could. They ended up focusing mainly on pecans and scrap metal.

SM: And you studied engineering at Tulane? WK: For whatever reason I was always really good at math and science. My grandmother used to make long division problems for me, and I used to always ask for bigger ones. I was interested in math and science from a very young age. I also played with Legos all the time. I still love Legos. I have two new nephews, and soon one of them will be getting Legos to play with.

In high school I had good chemistry, physics, and math teachers. That helped direct my skills. Initially I thought I was going to go to business school. I was accepted to the University of Chicago, but when I got to Tulane I found it more appealing for a guy who was 17. I thought I was going to be a stock broker – I'd been paper trading since I was 14. Eventually though I ended up declaring an engineering major.

SM: What happened when you got your degree? WK: Chemical engineering is a very cyclical degree. Probably not as much as it used to be, but it was tied to the petroleum industry, and back then oil was $14 a barrel. It was a very different environment, and it would go through booms and busts. When I entered university the cycle was at the top, and when I graduated it was at the bottom. The oil companies were not hiring.

I ended up taking a job for URS Consultants doing air permitting for the oil companies and chemical plants on the Mississippi River between New Orleans and Baton Rouge. I graduated on Friday and started work on Monday. That was the only offer I had, and it was a take-it-or-leave-it offer.

SM: How long did you work there? WK: Five months. The money was so bad that when I saw an ad in the paper for Schlumberger, I applied. I took their aptitude test, and they offered me a position as a field engineer. I did four months of training and went out and ran a crew of three or four guys in the Gulf of Mexico. We had about $3 million in equipment and took boats and choppers out to the oil platforms. I did that for about three years and ended up leaving burned out. The schedule was two weeks on, one week off, but that actually used to go more like 16 days on, 5 days off. It was tough to have a life with that job. I met my wife while I was working for them. I wanted to get more serious with her, so I left and interviewed for a company that was a joint venture between Exxon Chemical Americas and Nalco/Exxon Energy Chemicals.

I started with them in July of 1995, working in the field, technical support and sales. I had the opportunity to be involved in the early trials of a new technology. We were basically selling chemicals and providing solutions to fouling problems in the chemical industry on the process side, not on the water side. These specialized chemicals helped reduce rates of fouling and let the equipment run longer to save customers money.

SM: What was unique about what you were doing? How did it change the environment you were operating in? WK: This particular product was different because we put it in the inlet of an ethylene furnace, which can be 1,800–2,000 degrees Fahrenheit. That is a very tough environment to work in from a chemical standpoint. But it was a successful test project, and they eventually gave me an opportunity to come into corporate marketing. At the time, I was the youngest person to get into corporate marketing in the history of the company. I couldn't turn it down. We moved from New Orleans to Houston to accept the promotion in 1998.

I worked in that position, then took on some compressor anti-foulant products. I was working those two products for a while doing international business development. I was flying all over the world; I had potential customers on every continent but Antarctica. Having lived in Mississippi, I wanted to travel and see the world. It was great to do it on someone else's dime.

I was flying in and out of the Middle East before 9/11, looking down at all the water from the plane.

> *I remember seeing a* **National Geographic** *drawing of a big ocean device to create energy, and I kept thinking that there had to be some way to make energy out of those waves. That's how it started.*

At Exxon one of the things we did was mine the patent database to see where competitors were going with similar products. I applied that same approach to research on some theoretical big device out in the waves. The more I got into it, the more I realized there was a lot of intellectual property in the public domain. I saw a big gap in current-based hydrokinetics.

SM: Can you set the landscape in context a bit? WK: There are two ways to make energy from moving water. The motion of water is hydrokinetic, as opposed to head-based hydropower, where water is stored and released at a pressure head like you see with a dam. Within hydrokinetics, there are current-based hydrokinetics and wave-based hydrokinetics. In the wave-based hydrokinetic space, a lot of companies were looking at buoys and devices that worked on the motion of the water. A lot of them centered around an oscillating water column, which is where you trap air around a wave and a turbine. The wave pushes the air in and out of the turbine, causing it to spin and generate electricity.

There was not a lot of activity in the current-based hydrokinetic space. This is applicable where you have a river or an ocean current, or in a tidal area. In 2001 there were only one or two companies globally that were even looking at this approach.

SM: Did you even have a background in hydrokinetics? WK: I did not. In chemical engineering we think of ourselves as the best of the best.

SM: All engineers in all disciplines do! WK: I know! Chemical engineers do a lot of everything. You get exposed to mechanical engineering, statics, and dynamics. You learn about fluid flow.

SM: So you had enough of a background to make sense of the landscape? WK: Absolutely. I decided to take a Pareto chart to see what the issues were and why no technologies had come to the marketplace. I developed seven key parameters I thought prevented any technology from making it to the marketplace. When I started trying to create my design, I was running off those seven issues.

I left Exxon in 2001, filed a patent in 2002, and spent most of that year working on the ideas. I was working to find holes in the patent database. Retrospectively, I think we've done a pretty good job of that. We had an IP strategy law firm review our patents on behalf of some of the venture capitalists interested in investing in us. It's a very broad and strong patent that should be quite valuable in the future. Over the years we've expanded into different devices and designs, as well as ways to increase power output.

SM: What was it like quitting Exxon? Was it scary? WK: Well, I was actually fired. I had tried to do a buyout of a technology there, and had arranged money from Wall Street to do that. So they identified me as a troublemaker. One day, at the end of 2001, I was simply asked to pack up and leave. So, I had some soul searching to do. The idea was already starting to come together, so I decided to go for it. It was very difficult to chase financing in cleantech in 2002–2003. The market had completely dried up.

> SM: *Long journey alone!* WK: *Very long journey alone. People just don't understand why you're missing out on the best part of your life. People think it's a complete waste of time. My uncle told me so.*

SM: **How did your wife react?** WK: She was patient. Early on, it was very rough for her. As we started seeing some success, it became easier.

SM: **What did you do when you got the patent in October of 2005?** WK: I kissed it! Then I put it in the bank vault. And I sent a copy to my uncle who said all along that this wouldn't work.

On a more serious note, I started focusing on the financial model and the business plan. I think it was on version 12 by then. I joined the National Hydropower Association and went to their conference in March of 2006. At that point I had raised some funding from friends and family, and I started asking around for good companies who could do hydropower analysis for us. We hired Hatch Energy for some feasibility studies.

In early 2007 Hatch felt we were at the limit of what we could do. We needed to do some computational fluid dynamics. We went up and saw American Hydro in York, Pennsylvania – they're conventional head-based turbine designers. We went to see if they would have any interest in helping us with the computational fluid dynamics design, but at the time they were so busy they didn't have any spare time to help. Eventually, we went to Concepts NREC in Massachusetts, who were interested in helping us. We had raised a little more money by that point, which helped.

SM: Where did you raise the money from? WK: Mostly friends and family.

SM: Not your uncle! WK: No. The first investor put in $100,000; the second, who was a very good friend from college, put in $250,000. We had someone put in another $50,000, then a group that did $25,000 and $100,000. They were all doctors up until we did our Series A round. This was all in 2006–2007.

SM: What were you going to do with the turbine manufacturers you had approached? WK: When you measure flow in piping systems, you do it with ventures and pressure differentials. At the throat of a venture the velocity increases. Depending upon the approach and departure angles as well as the fluid type, you can control those velocities. I envisioned a design for a device that could get into the water to assist in water acceleration. It would allow for the turbine to be placed at the throat, where the water velocity was highest, and extract the greatest amount of energy. I had conceptual drawings of my thoughts, and those are what I took to Concepts NREC so they had an idea of where we were headed. I just needed an engineering firm to do the design and put the nuts and bolts together.

They did a feasibility level study, which looked good. They liked the idea of the different application points for the technology. We're now wrapping up the first commercial project, the first licensed project in the US.

SM: How did you get that project? WK: Chuck Alsberg from the National Hydropower Association made some introductions for me. Chuck was an *Atlas Shrugged* kind of a guy whom I had a good fit with. I was drawn to his character, and he liked what I was doing. He knew what he was doing, and he certainly knew a lot more than my uncle about what I was doing.

I had looked at different states to see where the production tax credits were highest. In Minnesota they have a 2.5 cent per kilowatt hour state production tax credit. There's also a federal production tax credit for incremental hydropower, although my technology had never been tried or applied as an incremental hydropower ignition. We went to seven different dam operators and did some inspections and surveys in Minnesota. The Army Corp of Engineers Locking Dam No. 2 was operated by the city of Hastings, and after surveying the dam, that became our focus.

I got in touch with the head of the city's public works, Tom Montgomery, and spoke with him about what we were doing. He was a big supporter right off the bat. They were willing to let us use their license and modify it, but could not come out of pocket for anything. It's all been done with our equipment, and we've paid for everything.

SM: How many people did you have helping on this? WK: It was just me. Toward the end of 2007, and in early 2008, I was out of funding and running on fumes. As we progressed into 2008, Mike Draper approached me, and I related the studies, the engineering, and the work behind it.

SM: How did Mike find you? WK: By doing a Google search for "hydro renewable." It was a pure coincidence.

He had just finished a solar investment and was looking for the next generation renewable in water. I walked into the office on January 5th or 6th, and received the phone call from Mike. We had an hour-and-a-half conversation. The more questions I heard, the more I realized there was genuine interest.

SM: How much money did you take in your Series A? WK: I took $2.6 million from Mike and Quercus Trust. I had other offers. I had some offers at $5 million and $6.7 million. I said no to those for a variety of reasons. It was a gut-wrenching decision and a huge leap of faith, but I felt that Mike really believed in me and the project.

SM: Are you actually powering a plant right now? WK: We've done prototypes, but the project in Hastings will be the first commercially licensed product.

SM: It's an existing plant that you're retrofitting with your technology, correct? WK: Right. We benefit from the clean water coming through. We have a patent that lets us capture wasted energy and create an additional system around it. It's only 12 feet in diameter but has a capacity of 100 kilowatts, which is enough to power 100 homes. We're going to put two units in Hastings, which will be a 5.7% increase of their base capacity.

SM: How much of the US energy capacity is hydropower? WK: Anywhere from 7% to 8%, which is 120,000 megawatts. Of all of that, approximately 50% is privately owned and operated, and the rest is operated by the federal government. What we would like to do, if we can get our leaders in DC to see the vision, is to get the federal government to retrofit and utilize the existing infrastructure. Typically, states have removable portfolio standards, and in a lot of states conventional hydro is not recognized. We're working to educate our leaders in DC.

We believe we're as environmentally friendly as solar and geothermal, and we can also make a big impact on America's energy independence.

SM: Do you think the 5% increase at Hastings will be representative of most other potential projects? WK: That depends on the type of facility. Some hydro facilities are very high energy, but it may be a product of the amount of flow as well as the elevation of the water used for generation. Some bring water down hills, which gives them huge leverage. In those cases we may only get a 1% increase in efficiency. Regardless, it is additional capacity.

SM: You said 8% of America's energy is hydro. Could that number change with a broad deployment of your technology? WK: The potential easily exists to increase US capacity by 20%. The Department of Energy did a head-based hydro study in which they said there were 185,000 megawatts of potential additional hydro out there.

SM: Outside of the US, hydropower is viewed in a positive light; here it has a stigma. Why is this? WK: I think there have been a number of large lawsuits brought by the environmental community over the years that the government has lost. They've dealt with the health of the ecosystem and the Endangered Species Act. People don't realize all the benefits of hydropower. First, hydropower provides emission-free renewable energy. Second, it provides recreation in the form of lakes people can boat on. Third, in many cases it provides irrigation and drinking supply. Our technology is very fish friendly. We recognized from the very beginning that fish were the issue with hydro, so our initial design parameters were to have 100% fish survivability.

SM: How did you do that? WK: Our design only rotates at 21 rpm, more like a revolving door at the airport. You could literally swim through our turbine.

SM: What is your business model? Do you get a percentage of the extra power generated? WK: For Hastings we have a power purchase agreement with the city. We get a percentage of the revenue that comes from power generation. More than likely, as we go forward, we would do it as an equipment sale since it's a patented system that can bring royalty back to the company.

We also have some greenfield projects we're trying to do on our own. In that case we would be the power operator and negotiate a power purchase agreement with the end users. We have a number of projects in Alaska where remote towns are off the grid and use diesel to generate power. The equivalent cost per kilowatt hour can be 74–80 cents an hour. The state of Alaska gives rebates for some of that, but the end user still sees 20 cents or more per kilowatt hour for their power cost.

SM: Operationally, how is the company working? Who manufactures the equipment? WK: Our first unit is being manufactured via various sites. Our engineering firm is the project manager, and we're going to assemble it onsite. As we go forward our strategy is to use contract manufacturing. We've already been in discussions with an automobile manufacturer that doesn't have as much business as they had in the past. They have plants here in the US and Canada, and they already do some manufacturing for renewable energy companies. They have the skill set to do not only manufacturing, but assembly as well.

SM: Now you need big dollars. WK: Exactly. We're in due diligence with five firms at this point, and it looks like we'll receive the funding we need. We have a New York Stock Exchange EPC company acting as a strategic lead. It's an interesting group because it brings in the core disciplines we need such as manufacturing, design, and knowledge of application points where we can deploy this technology in the future.

SM: How are you dealing with valuation issues between your first round and your next round? WK: We're doing it based on contracts that are being negotiated. We also have a nice pipeline. By the end of 2009 we should have $20 million on the books in sales. Recurring revenue is also generated from power purchase agreements.

When we go to existing hydro facilities and do the non-capacity amendment to the license, we expect FERC to issue the license for the remainder of the existing license. In the case of Hastings, they have 23 years left on their license, so this should be in for 23 years. We'll also be first to market in the US with a FERC-issued license for hydrokinetic generation. We're getting first-mover advantage, revenue generation in Q4 2008, and a number of potential $5–$10 million projects that have the possibility of closing in Q4 2008. We have a nice pipeline and a lot of interest from Europe and Kyoto Protocol countries that have emission reduction targets.

SM: Sounds like you have good traction and have made those first four years start paying off! Congratulations.

WEAPON OF MASS RECONSTRUCTION

As Barack Obama works out his policies to stimulate the US economy, he needs to invest some intellectual firepower in understanding the needs of bootstrapping entrepreneurs. Such people don't need the boatloads of money traditional venture capital brings, but by creating income and jobs, they can become a powerful weapon for mass reconstruction.

I remain resolute that if entrepreneurs the world over learn to build sustainable small businesses without requiring large amounts of outside financing, the global economy will run without a hitch. No doubt, many of these ventures will go on to seek large-scale expansion capital, in building out larger enterprises, but those who don't grow exponentially will still enjoy the pride and privilege of being small business owners. And we as people, and we as communities and as nations, will enjoy the health and wealth of their contributions.

One of my favorite stories of innovation is that of Scott Wainner of Dallas, Texas, who at 15 years old started an online community. "I was really big on trying to tweak the performance of my computer, so I started SysOpt.com as a way to reach out to other people and get their help tweaking my computer." The year: 1994. A year before Netscape went public. Talk about a precocious kid!

By 1999, SysOpt had grown to 500,000 unique users and several million page views per month without any marketing investment. The magic of the Internet took over. As it was years before Google launched its now famous AdSense network, Wainner sold ads himself. He sold the first banner ad for $25 a month, but within five years his once small online community business had become a $100,000-a-year cash cow. The only investment: an inordinate portion of Wainner's personal time.

Soon, young Scott Wainner had to make a choice. His dream of becoming an aerospace engineer had propelled him to seek admission at Texas A&M University, but by his sophomore year, what had started as a hobby was generating serious cash and demanding more and more of his time.

Wainner dropped out, moved to Portland, Oregon, and focused full-time on his budding entrepreneurial career. He launched another site, ResellerRatings.com, where people reviewed various online retailers.

At the height of the dotcom frenzy, acquisition offers started surfacing. "I went out on my balcony and screamed; I was just 20 years old," recounts Wainner, with the keen perspective of age (he's now 29). Eventually, EarthWeb bought both SysOpt and ResellerRatings. It was a strange negotiation, near gunpoint, the way Wainner tells it. "We'll give you a $350,000 cash bonus if you sign our offer today," he recalls acquirers telling him, "but if you walk out of the office, that's it."

Not everything went well after the sale to EarthWeb. Eventually, Wainner bought back ResellerRatings.com, and within a year, revitalized it into a thriving community, generating $1 million a year in revenue. That was 2004. Today, the site generates a couple million dollars a year in revenue.

What surprises him still is how much money he sees sloshing around in startups. "I look at some of these sites that have received $10 million in funding, and I wonder what they're doing with all that money. I don't need it. I do it slower. For me, being an entrepreneur is so much trial and error that I would rather make the mistakes in the lower dollar range than at the Super Bowl advertising level."

What Wainner's story embodies is the incredible wealth-creation opportunity that the Internet offers to bootstrapped entrepreneurship. Not every company needs to be a Google; entrepreneurs can build lifestyle businesses, family businesses, cash businesses. They might not generate enough returns to fund union pension funds or university sports stadiums – and so are ignored by mainstream venture business – but they do generate enough to offer more than a decent livelihood.

On the other hand, some homegrown companies do balloon into venture-funded enterprises, as Ramu Yalamanchi's hi5 did. Also a bootstrapped online community, San Francisco–based hi5 took six months to hit the million-user mark. Today, it's adding a million users a week and is the No. 1 social media site in Portugal as well as much of Spanish-speaking Latin America.

While Facebook and MySpace conquered the US market, hi5 quietly staked out an enviable position in the international markets with simple, yet profound, touches. "We thought about little things like colors. In certain countries, certain colors have certain meanings. Black has a connotation in the US, as does purple in Thailand," says Yalamanchi.

Hi5 hit five million registered users by the end of its launch year, 2004; by 2005, 20 million. It now boasts more than 80 million registered members – all funded by a paltry $250,000 from genuine friends and family.

Both Wainner and Yalamanchi have created great businesses – great for their customers, their employees, and the economy as a whole. The world needs these kinds of bootstrappers. Let's hope President Obama knows how much we need them, too.

Scott Wainner, SysOpt and ResellerRatings

Close your eyes for a moment and think back to what you were doing at 15 years of age. Surviving trigonometry? Delivering newspapers? How many of us can say we started an Internet business? Well, that's what Scott Wainner did.

In the years since, Scott has accumulated enormous business experience by starting, selling, buying back, and rebuilding ventures. What sounds like a 30-year resume is, in fact, half that. Someday soon, Scott will be 30.

SM: I would like to start by asking about your background. Where are you from? SW: I was born in Florida and grew up in Dallas. I was raised by my mom. In 1994 I started experimenting with BBS and early pre-Internet places. At the same time I started hearing about this Internet thing, and I really found it interesting.

SM: How old were you then? SW: Fifteen.

SM: Who told you about Internet bulletin boards? SW: There were free newspapers that had all of the bulletin board numbers; you'd just dial them up directly with a modem. There were sheets and sheets of numbers. They were good for utilities and things like that. In one of these publications there were ads for ISPs, and

I thought I should figure out this Internet thing.

I had an AOL account for 30 days. I then got my own dial-up account and used Netscape. I just started fooling around, and it wasn't long before I wanted to make my own site. I was big into aviation, so I played a lot of flight simulators. I didn't have any money, and I didn't come from a family that had a lot of money, so I didn't have a good computer. I would play these simulators, and the frame rate would be really choppy and unrealistic. I was really big on trying to tweak the performance of my computer, so I started SysOpt.com as a way to reach out to other people and get their help tweaking my computer. That was in 1994.

SM: This was a community where people who were interested in speeding up their computers were engaging with each other? SW: Yes, it was a very early forum. I would write articles and ask for advice from people. The main draw of the site was that everyone would post their performance benchmark ratings for their computers. We would compare and compete. We were also big into overclocking. Intel would set their computer chip at 200mhz, and we would run it at 266mhz. That was the beginning of SysOpt.

SM: How did the site get known? SW: Just word of mouth. I ran it as a hobby. I never put money into marketing it, and SEO wasn't even a thing. Google wasn't even around yet.

SM: How many people were on the site? SW: By 1999 it had grown to several million page views a month. There were probably 500,000 unique users. It grew rapidly. This was before AdSense, so there was no ad network organized. I went out to individual companies and got some simple advertising. I sold my first banner ad for $25 a month. From the time I launched until 1999 the site was making about $100,000 a year in ad revenue.

SM: Did you do SysOpt.com full-time, or was it just on the side? SW: When I was in high school I worked on it after school as a hobby. When it started to pass the $30,000, $40,000, and $60,000 a year mark, I started to think there could be something good going on. I was really still interested in aviation. I had this great Internet thing going on, but I wanted to be an aviation engineer. I went to Texas A&M when I was 17 to be an aerospace engineer.

I started studying engineering and ran the business, which was earning more than $100,000, on the side. It was taking a lot of my time, and I was faced with tough classes like calculus that did not come naturally for me. By my sophomore year I decided to leave school for a while and just focus on the business. That was during the early days of the craziness.

I had a friend in Portland, Oregon, who was an entrepreneur like me, and we had done some work together, so I moved. I had been chatting with him, and he invited me up to do some windsurfing. I left school – I was never a big school person. I was always focused on the business stuff. I went to the guidance counselors, who asked if I was really sure I wanted to do this, and I told them I was positive.

SM: Did you tell the guidance counselors how much money you were making? SW: No, but they wouldn't have believed it. They would have thought I was dealing drugs!

SM: The $100,000 a year you were making at the time all came via advertising? SW: Yes. Initially I reached out to companies I thought would be a good fit. There was an early ad network called Commonwealth which would stick their code on your site and pay you a CPM. After 1997 and 1998 they gave a decent payout. I also partnered with a guy in Canada who made a diagnostic card that people could use to troubleshoot their computers. I sold that through the site as well, which accounted for part of the revenue. I would also seek out individual companies to stick banner ads on the site.

Somewhere in there I launched ResellerRatings.com. It was part of SysOpt at first, but eventually it went on its own. It was my selfish way of trying to find online retailers that I could trust. There was nothing like that at the time. There was no BizRate or RatingsSource. I never knew if I could trust an online store. It was a place for people to write and read reviews, and for people to leave their opinions. At first it didn't earn any money but a couple thousand dollars a year from merchant ads. ResellerRatings and SysOpt both grew, and in 1999 I started getting into the sellout craze.

SM: How did the sellout craze affect you? Were people coming to you trying to buy your site? SW: I had been in Portland for a couple months when out of the blue I got an e-mail from Andover, the company that bought SlashDot and was later acquired by VA Linux. They asked if they could partner with me. I returned their e-mail asking what they wanted to do, and their answer was that they wanted to buy the site. Their response e-mail included an offer which shocked me. I don't remember what it was, but it was several hundred thousand in cash, plus stock and other benefits. I was doing well but had only saved about $30,000 at the time, so it was tempting.

SM: They wanted to buy SysOpt or ResellerRatings.com? SW: They offered to buy both as a packaged deal. I was on cloud nine. I went out on my balcony and screamed; I was just 20 years old. I had my head down in the business operations, so I was unaware of the bubble stuff going on. Then it dawned on me that there were some crazy valuations happening. I realized I needed to look into the offer in more detail. I didn't have any business training, and I had no other offer to compare it to, so I had no idea if that was even a good price.

I started reaching out to contacts, trying to seek another bidder. If I could get another bidder, I could get into a bidding war. It didn't take long at all. People recommended I contact EarthWeb, which was the company that I eventually sold to. They expressed interest right away and made me an offer that was 30–40% larger than the Andover offer. I then started playing them against each other in a very amateurish way. It worked, though. EarthWeb asked me to come out to the New York office and talk about the deal. Andover said if I was going to New York I should just stop by Massachusetts and talk to them as well.

I planned a trip and visited both companies. EarthWeb was spending cash like crazy; a lot of companies were. They had just gone public, so they had a lot of cash. They had an entire floor of this 50-story Manhattan building – the view was amazing. I was up there sitting with them in a conference room, and they were mapping out the strategy of their earn-out proposal on the whiteboard. They said, "We'll give you a $350,000 cash bonus if you sign our offer today, but if you walk out of the office, that's it." They had also offered me more money and more stock. I had planned to meet with Andover later in the day, and I was thinking I should call Andover to see if they would top it. But I couldn't get in touch with the Andover people, so I decided to just do it.

I also heard that some of their folks were going to fly on a Gulfstream jet they had chartered from New York to San Francisco for a road show. I joked that if they would let me ride back to California on their jet, I'd sign the deal. They said sure, so I got to ride in the cockpit of this jet on a $20,000 flight. There were two takeoffs and landings; it was awesome. It was an amazing experience for a 20-year-old with no business training. My hobby paid well.

SM: How old are you now? SW: 29.

SM: And the last nine years?

> SW: *The high point was the sale to EarthWeb, and it went downhill from there.*

The first few months they gave me $20,000 a month to run the site. Half of the purchase price was based on a traffic-based earnout. I had to hit certain targets at years one, two, and three. In hindsight, that was a huge mistake. Due to the earnout, EarthWeb had an obligation to support the site no less favorably than their other sites. When they started going south, things got bad. Out of the blue they sold all of their properties, including my sites, to Internet.com. The only site they maintained was Dice.com, and they essentially became Dice.com.

I was flipping out because they had no right to reassign the asset purchase agreement and the earnout obligations they had signed with me to another company. I told them they owed me the earnout because they had messed everything up. Of course, Internet.com acquired the site and reduced the budget from $20,000 to $2,000. I didn't know how I was supposed to get the earnout after that. ResellerRatings was caught up in all of this as well. It was smaller than SysOpt and did not make as much money. Internet.com did not understand the model, so it was pushed off to the side very quickly.

After a few months of the $2,000 budget, they said they were going to lay me off completely. I now had no ability to affect the sites. EarthWeb was telling me that I didn't hit the traffic metrics for the first year, and Internet.com is on the hook for years two and three. I was asking them how they knew I didn't hit the traffic for year one –

they weren't recording the traffic well. It was just a huge mess. I was upset about the earnout, and I was threatening legal action.

SM: You got your original bonuses, so financially you were OK, right? SW: I got cash and stock. The stock was a mess. I couldn't sell the stock they gave me for one year, and by then the crash had happened. The cash I got was good. I also had the earn-out lined up, but they weren't willing to pay me. In a way I kind of knew going into it that the earnout was risky. It was icing on the cake. I was not really depending on it; however, it was there and was something I wanted to get because it was a lot of money.

A few months later, probably late 2001, out of the blue they decided to shut down ResellerRatings completely. They put up a splash page saying, "Sorry, ResellerRatings.com has been discontinued." The site had a few hundred thousand unique users, a community, and people were really mad about that. I immediately wrote them asking if I could buy the site back. They offered to sell it for $500,000. I came back and said, "OK, you paid $500,000 for all of EarthWeb's properties a few months before. There is no way I am paying $500,000 for that single property back. I will let you out of the earnout obligation you inherited from EarthWeb, because legally I believe you owe me money, if you give me ResellerRatings and SysOpt back free."

They came back and said they would not do that. However, they said if I let them out of the earnout, they would sell me ResellerRatings.com for mid–five figures. I decided to go ahead and buy it. My lawyer, a great guy in New York, told me not to release them from the earnout because it was a bad deal. Internet.com's lawyer was jumping up and down saying the deal had to be done today, or the deal was dead. It was crazy, very emotional, insanity. It was the only time I have ever gone against the advice of my lawyer, and I'm glad I did.

SM: I think you were right. SW: Well, at least I was the proud owner of my site once again.

SM: The site was shut down while you were negotiating the purchase? SW: It was only down for a couple of weeks, thankfully, so it wasn't damaged too much. There were a few articles written saying that ResellerRatings.com was gone. It was unique; I don't know too many Web sites that just plain shut down.

I wondered why they did that, and the only thing I could think of was that merchants were complaining about the users' ratings, and Internet.com didn't want the headache.

SM: When you took it back, did you tell the community what you had just gone through? SW: I told them I had repurchased the site, but not what I had gone through to do it.

I inherited a site that had been neglected. Both EarthWeb and Internet.com told me not to work on the site. ResellerRatings.com really does run itself because the content is user-generated, but the thing that does require maintenance is when merchants write in to disagree with a review. We've always had policies surrounding this – for example, we don't remove reviews unless they violate our policies. It does require maintenance, however, just to respond to all of the merchants. But for a period of time there had simply been no maintenance.

SM: So a lot of junk had accumulated. SW: Exactly. I had inherited a lot of junk. Part of the problem was that the site had old, sloppy Perl coding, and the database was flat file and had locking issues. It did not make money. The only positive thing was that it had traffic.

SM: What were users reviewing? Was there any particular type of merchandise? SW: They reviewed the reputations of online retailers. Because it was tied with SysOpt, it had an audience focused on electronics. When I bought the site back, I hired a couple young guys to revitalize it. I didn't have a lot of income because I had no business, so I couldn't afford to pay them that much. I told them I would pay a percentage of the revenue the business generated. The three of us reworked all the code, hired a Web designer to give the site a fresh look, and got rid of all the junk. We threw out reviews altogether where necessary. We replaced the back end with MySQL and started looking at monetization of the site. We partnered with Shopping.com to power the shopping engine component. We earned revenue through clicks and had CPC-based revenue. We just really started cleaning and growing from there.

SM: What kind of metrics did you get in the years after you took it back? SW: It was up to $1 million a year in 2004. That was mostly Shopping.com revenue. The people coming to the site to read reviews were shoppers. The targeted audience was shoppers, so it monetized really well. Traffic has grown over the years, but it isn't crazy growth. It has always been 400,000–500,000 unique users and a couple million page views. When I bought it there were about 100,000 users.

SM: Where are your traffic levels today? SW: We have about 600,000 uniques and a couple million page views.

SM: Where are you in terms of revenue? SW: A couple million dollars a year.

SM: Much of the comparison shopping industry on the Internet is reviewing products, whereas you're reviewing the retailers. Is that the big differentiation? SW: It is. ResellerRatings has always been in this weird niche. Most merchant reviews are only found on shopping engines like Shopping.com.

> *We're positioned uniquely because we do not allow opt-in. Merchants will be listed in ResellerRatings whether they like it or not, and often they do not like it.*

This is not the case for Shopping.com – if you don't pay them to be in their engine, you aren't going to be rated in their engine. We're a lot less biased on reviews. We have 15,000 stores, many of which are little stores you'll not find reviewed anywhere else.

SM: Where do you go from here? You have a $2 million business and six people. SW: I started looking a lot more into the bargains and deals space and not just in the merchant review space. I think for ResellerRatings there is a lot of opportunity for merchants, such as giving them tools to manage their feedback, which we do. We have free and premium tools that let merchants get into the process to see who is writing reviews. For ResellerRatings, something I realized a long time ago is that there isn't a buzz about the site in terms of people checking it frequently. They use it as a tool, and it's a great tool, but they only use it when they need to. I've been looking at ways to create a site that's a bit more addictive, a site that someone has to visit every day.

That's where Dealighted.com came in. That was in late 2006. I was visiting sites like SlickDeals and FatWallet as well as bargain shopping sites, and I was looking at their forums. There are thousands of deals posted to the forums every day, and it's impossible to figure out which deals are active and which are expired. The front page could be some deal that's six months old. So I identified an opportunity to weed through all of that. It would literally be an eight-hour-a-day job to look at a thousand deals a day. Aggregators think it's a great idea to aggregate and just barf it out to you. But that does not solve the problem.

I took the aggregation component and sorted it. I don't do it in a Digg style where people vote; I just use the data that's already out there. I took data like reply data, how active the views are, the ratings people give to deals, and pulled all of this data to look at the deals posted today and say which are junk and which are hot. The hot deals get posted to the top of the Dealighted page.

The site is growing like crazy. In December 2007 it got 300,000 visits, which should've been really high, but in June 2008 it got 650,000 visits. People are visiting multiple times, getting addicted.

SM: Is your monetization the same Shopping.com model?
SW: It is the same model. On top of that, we benefit from things like WidgetBucks, where they're using Shopping.com-type products, putting ad placements on sites, and benefiting from the CPCs. That's something we did a while ago. We use our Shopping.com data and product feeds to figure out which products are hot. We then pay sites for ad space, and we stick these products there in ad blocks. We get the CPCs when people click on these products, and we pay the sites a flat rate.

We use those ads on other sites and on ResellerRatings. There's a conversion loss on ResellerRatings: when a person searches for something, she may click all the way through to a merchant or she may not. We use these ads as a way to cut out that conversion. The ad is right there, and when a person clicks on it there's no loss.

SM: Can you talk about the six people who work with you? Where did you find them? How did that team come together? SW: I am really bad at hiring people. I can create, innovate, and grow. But when I encounter something repetitive that I do not want to keep doing, I hire someone to do that. I am really bad at finding people who are clones of me, who can innovate and grow. The people I have working for me have always come to me, and when I've sought out people it has never gone that well. Most people I hire are fans of the site. I hire them in a small role at first, then grow it from there.

> *SM: Your ventures make a lot of large, highly capitalized companies look bloated and obsolete. It's classic bootstrapping. SW: True. I look at some of these sites that have received $10 million in funding, and I wonder what they're doing with all that money. I don't need it. I do it slower. For me, being an entrepreneur is so much trial and error that I would rather make the mistakes in the lower dollar range than at the Super Bowl advertising level.*

SM: Is there anything I should've asked, but didn't? SW: There are other businesses I created along the way. After Internet. com laid me off, I started TechIMO. I wanted to figure out how to get those people [at SysOpt] to come over to something new. The TechIMO site was basically a clone of SysOpt. It was a forum that had the same focus, and I contacted just a few people. Word of mouth spread fast, and everyone left SysOpt and came over. Internet.com really lost out because there were thousands of active users who came over to TechIMO. It's growing like crazy — it's not able to monetize nearly as well as ResellerRatings because it's a tech forum, but it's getting about 750,000 visits a month.

In 2001 I had this TechIMO site, and people were asking for a photo gallery. There was certainly nothing that worked with vBulletin, so I decided to create a photo gallery and integrate with vBulletin. People started finding the photo gallery and asking me where I got it. After enough inquiries I cleaned it up, packaged it, and made it available for sale. It's PHP and MySQL and works with vBulletin, which was the main selling point at the time.

We have about 12,000 Web sites that use PhotoPost, and we sell it for about $100 a license. There are annual support fees and renewal fees that can take that up to $130. It's still just a photo gallery. I read your article about Web 3.0 and photo sharing, and I think there's a way to make PhotoPost a player among the photo sharing sites.

SM: Well, I look forward to it. What an interesting story. Congratulations!

Ramu Yalamanchi, hi5

Ramu Yalamanchi tried his hands at entrepreneurship multiple times, on each occasion taking away bits and pieces of what he needed. This time around, with hi5, it seems Ramu has put it all together.

Like myself, Ramu grew up as an entrepreneur's son, and enjoyed the luxury of being able to dialog with his father on business issues. His father also gave him the first $10,000 to start hi5. Today, though, I wonder whether it is the father who asks his son for business advice.

SM: Ramu, let's start by discussing some of your personal history. RY: I grew up in the western suburbs of Chicago. My dad has been an entrepreneur for as long as I can remember. He's an industrial engineer by training, and he probably worked until the time I was 10. He was always dabbling in different types of businesses. He used to have an auto shop before moving on to printing. Today he's more involved with real estate. One of the biggest things I learned from him was persistence.

> *No matter how many businesses you start, it just*
> *takes one successful business to make up for all the other*
> *attempts.*

Growing up, I remember Friday nights in particular. My dad would always come home with a story. He would talk about Steve Jobs, Bill Gates, and all these guys starting their companies. Even today when there's something in the business I need advice on, he's one of the first people I call.

At the University of Illinois I knew I wanted to become an entrepreneur, but I chose computer science because I realized from my dad that what industry you're in makes a big difference. I think Warren Buffet says this, too. If you're mediocre in finance, you'll do much better than if you're mediocre in the printing business. So I studied computer science and graduated in 1996. Mosaic was developed at the University of Illinois in 1994. My last year of college I joined a group of guys, and we started a company doing auctions for online advertising.

SM: Were they friends you grew up with in Chicago? RY: Two of them are from Chicago, the other was from Missouri. It ended up being an interesting group. Two of them started PayPal, and the other had a company purchased by Microsoft. Everyone has gone on to start interesting companies. That company in itself was not a huge success, but we all learned a ton. After that I wanted to come to Silicon Valley and learn all the things I didn't know.

I decided to get jobs that would help me fill the gaps. The first company I worked at was called ClickOver. I did sales and business development for a couple years. It was a very interesting experience. They sold to CMGi in the summer of 1998. I then joined eGroups — that's where I learned product management, which I felt was crucial to learning how to start my own company.

SM: After working in some of the functional positions, you felt confident you could leverage your experience with a startup of your own? RY: Yes. Unfortunately, I was overconfident. I jumped back into starting companies, but I still had some learning to do. I started a company which provided an underlying technology similar to what AJAX does today. It was a plug-in users would download, and developers could provide rich Internet applications on top of the plug-in. I raised a small amount of money for it and ran it for a year, but the company didn't go anywhere. After that I started a customer support company providing a hosted e-mail solution to consumer companies. I got the business to the point where it was slightly profitable, but I realized it would take a long time to make it a big business. Through this I learned I have to do things where my passion lies. I was not passionate about enterprise software.

SM: What did you do with that company? RY: I didn't have investors. It was entirely bootstrapped, so I just stopped running it.

SM: That brought you to hi5 in July 2002. What was the genesis of the idea? RY: I really wanted to get back into consumer-facing applications. At that time the Web was good at being a publishing model. The idea of using the Web for collaboration, communication, and getting people to do that through more than e-mail and instant messaging was new. Those were some of the things I was thinking about. I was also thinking about the growth of Internet users beyond the US. It seemed there was huge opportunity internationally.

The first way we started to take advantage of that was by replicating what Match.com did. I thought there was an opportunity to do the same thing internationally. I built a competitor to Match.com and launched it in the beginning of 2003. I did that for about four or five months and quickly realized it was not the kind of business I wanted to be in long term. It was a turn model. The media was used to acquire users, who stayed for three months, then moved on.

SM: Was that when Friendster was going? RY: Friendster had launched in early 2003, I believe. There were a lot of lessons from that as well. If you look at search, social networking, and a bunch of similar categories, they all seem to go through evolutions. Friendster was first generation. Some of the things we learned from them were that scale really matters.

> *If you're going to build a service and it has a good chance of becoming very popular, make sure you address the scale needs up front.*

SM: In your analysis, was that their main problem? RY: I don't know enough about what was happening inside the company, but externally there was a big problem. Users could not get to the site and could not register. They couldn't log into the site as often as they wanted.

Scale is really a simplified version of the problem. It really comes down to how they approached the problem, the technology used, and the product provided. The organization needs to be focused on the goals for success and what the usage is going to be. There may be other things as well. I think they were trying to do a lot early on. The lesson I've learned from many businesses is *focus*. Both picking the businesses initially, and deciding the order of areas to pursue.

SM: What business did you think you were getting into in 2003? RY: The business we thought we were getting into could broadly be defined as communication. We thought we were providing an option beyond what people were doing with e-mail and instant messaging. Over time, new methods of communication have continually been invented. It just seemed like there was a potential for a more fluid Web-based communication.

Another reason we thought it was interesting was that this enabled real people, as it happened millions of people, to get published on the Web. At the time there wasn't a single place you could go to and get a relevant stream of content from all the people you knew. We saw this as a way to enhance personal communications.

SM: What happened after you launched? Where did you launch, and what kind of ramp did you see? RY: We launched in English for all markets. It took us six months to get our first million members. Today we add a million members a week.

SM: How did you get your first million members? RY: It was all about the product. We built the product so that for users to get value out of it they needed to bring their friends into the service. In order to see their photos or communicate with them, users needed to draw their friends into hi5. This led to entirely organic growth.

SM: What did you learn about the usage patterns of the first million users? RY: They consumed a lot of photos. In terms of their profiles, there are a large number of categories. There are some who don't necessarily have thousands of friends, but they have a set of friends which numbers in the hundreds, and they use hi5 as a way to see what's happening in their lives.

> *There is another group of folks who are one way in real life, but very different on the social network. It's almost their alter ego. There's a user in Trinidad who has 15,000 friends on hi5. In real life he describes himself as spiritual, conservative, and shy. He's using hi5 as a way to find a different personality from his own, to be very social.*

There are folks that could be described as expressionists. They're on hi5 because they want to put up a lot of photos of themselves. They want the attention and are probably like that in real life as well. Yet another group uses hi5 as a tool. In Portugal we're the No. 2 site overall and the No. 1 social networking site. Bands and promoters use hi5 to let people know about events.

SM: What was the geographic distribution of your first million users? RY: About 80% of our users are outside the US. We saw growth go around the world. One of the first areas that grew fast was the Spanish-speaking markets. That led us to focus more on those markets.

SM: Your software was first out in English, right? RY: It was, but we saw traction in certain markets. The Spanish-speaking markets were adopting the English version of the software.

SM: How do you rank in Spanish-speaking countries? RY: We're the No. 1 social networking company.

SM: Do you have any idea why? RY: Because we targeted those demographics. We focused on Spanish-speaking users. There are many different ways to segment. There's behavioral segmentation, graphical segmentation, you name it. What we did was look at all of our users, observe their behaviors, and notice that behavior is not always the same from market to market. Spanish markets were more similar to each other. We were also doing things to support markets as a community. Early on in the business we localized the site and provided ways for them to meet people locally.

SM: Did you do that type of focusing for the first million users? RY: The first million were distributed, but we did look for patterns. We accumulated the first million users just as a function of them using the product. MySpace at the time was not letting non-US users register. They filtered users based on IP address. We took the opposite approach as we thought international markets were interesting markets.

SM: Were you the only option for international users at the time? RY: Friendster was very international. I believe some simple factors helped us though. Simple things about any Web service are important – things like how fast the site loaded internationally for all of our users. One of the first things we did very early on from a technical aspect was leverage content delivery networks. Today most social networks do this, but we did it fairly early. If consuming photos was a user's primary activity in Mexico City, then we became the best option, though not necessarily the only option.

Our design and our name have also helped create a great brand. In the category of social networking, brands mean something to the user. The fact that we have a simple name which is easy to brand helped. We also kept our design very simple so the page would load fast. We thought about little things like colors. In certain countries certain colors have certain meanings. Black has a connotation in the US, as does purple in Thailand.

SM: After the first six months and one million users, what kind of ramp did you experience? RY: It ramped faster and faster. It kept accelerating. We did one million in six months, then hit five million by the end of the first year. In 2005 we grew from five million to 20 million. In 2006 we went from 20 million to 40 million.

SM: Was this all still happening organically, or were you marketing at this point? RY: It was all still organic growth. There was no marketing expense.

SM: How did you fund the initial startup phase? RY: We had a rolling round, primarily from friends and family, with a target goal of $250,000. The first $10,000 came from my dad. I had gone to Chicago, where my brother had just started working as an internist. He wanted to introduce me to his friends because he wanted them to invest. I told him I wanted $250,000, and he told me it wouldn't be a problem. But I went there and made the pitch and left with just one of his friends investing $10,000. I went home and was pretty upset about that, so my dad gave me the next $10,000. He told me it would help me be successful!

The rest of the funds came from friends. I have a friend who put in $80,000. In April of 2004 we raised the last $50,000 of the initial $250,000 target. That allowed us to get the business profitable in October of 2004. The cost of delivering Web services was going down, so that worked in our favor. Bandwidth was going down, and servers were getting more efficient. At the same time ads were going up. We hit it at the opportune time.

SM: How did you ramp the ad sales? RY: We've always tried to stay pretty focused on product and product development. That led us to find interesting partnerships where we could outsource the ad sales. Early on in the business we worked with traditional ad networks, which included a division of Monster called Tickle, whom we still work with today. They've been a great partner, helping us monetize at a level that would have taken us 12 months or so to reach.

SM: What types of ads does Tickle serve to you? RY: They're an ad sales rep company. They go to consumer packaged goods and movie studios and get good brands on board. They're a rep firm.

SM: Were they filling your entire inventory? If you had five million users at the time, you had good volume. RY: They were not filling all of it. They were filling a decent amount of inventory. Today we do 20 billion pages a month and probably 30 billion ads a month. At the time it may have been a few million

ads a day. It was a much lower volume, but we were able to monetize it well enough that we could support the business.

SM: How have you seen ad rates work for your audience?
RY: They've gone up over time. That's a function of more dollars
coming to the Web as a whole.

> *Our next goal is to know more about the user and
> what the user actually wants so we can understand
> intent. That's how we think about the business going
> forward as opposed to 20 billion views of untargeted
> advertising.*

**SM: Beyond the demographic understanding, have your
revenues to date come from untargeted advertising?** RY: Revenues have come a few ways. One of the ways we've been able to
continue to monetize our inventory around the world is by using
the same model we started with. We had a really good partner in
the US, and we've expanded that to include companies in a half
dozen different countries throughout the world. We have a deal
with Portugal Telecom; we have a deal with one of the top Internet companies in Thailand; and we have many other similar deals.
These partnerships allow us to monetize at a level that would have
been difficult to do ourselves unless we'd gone out and built our
own sales teams.

**SM: A lot of rep firms have a reputation for having very
high commissions, often upwards of 60%. Are your rep firms
requiring commissions that high?** RY: No, they are not. It's a
volume and scale business. Compared to what it would cost us to
build and hold our own sales force, as a percentage of revenue, I
think we get close to those levels. That is especially true as we scale
bigger. It becomes competitive. It's as good as what the next rep
firm is willing to offer.

SM: Are your demographics teen driven? RY: That's a really interesting area, which I've been looking into. I'm fascinated not only by who uses social networks today but directionally, who will be using social networks 10 to 15 years into the future. Today the audience skews young. The 15–24 demographic is the largest audience. There's also significant representation in the 25–34 segment. After that it drops off.

It's very interesting to compare the growth in the 15–24 demographic in various markets. One data point is a comparison between us, Hotmail, and Yahoo! Mail. Between March 2007 and April 2008 we grew 81% in Mexico as measured by unique visits. In comparison, Hotmail grew 4%, and Yahoo! Mail declined.

When evaluating hi5's popularity as a percentage of usage days, we remain very strong. On average, people in Mexico go to the Web 12 times a month. We account for 47% of those visits. This correlates to another metric, time spent online. An average user in Mexico will spend 33 minutes on the Web, and 37% of that time is on hi5.

Directionally these metrics tell me two things. First, social networks, and specifically hi5, are becoming the means of personal communications.

> *People are still using e-mail for communication which is transactional in nature. But personal communications, keeping in touch and the "here's what I did last weekend" conversations, are moving to social networks.*

Second, in Mexico, we have the metrics to support this although we believe it is true for all of the other markets as well – it appears hi5 is the driving reason people come back to the Web. The number of times they return to the Web in a month, and the percentage of the time spent on hi5 during those return visits, tells us that we are a key reason people in many areas use the Internet.

SM: Traditionally, I would say e-mail is the key reason people use the Web, but if personal communications are migrating to social networks, then what you say makes sense. RY: Your initial question was about age. What I see happening over time is that the 15–24 demographic will one day become the 25–34 demographic, and when they do they're going to continue to communicate using hi5. Social networking today looks like a young phenomenon. But over time it's going to become increasingly widespread.

SM: Social networks are becoming the voice of a generation. RY: Exactly! Another thing to think about is that people are fundamentally social. What is happening online is a reflection of social behavior in the real world. Sites like ours are just enhancing natural behavior.

SM: Where are you in terms of revenue? RY: We don't talk about the actual financials. We brought the company to profitability in October of 2004 and ran it profitably through 2007 when we raised capital.

SM: Why did you raise capital? RY: To enable expansion. We were investing in the business based on profits anticipated in the next 90 days. It was not a long-term view. I believe that social networks will become the top sites in every country. And to continue to develop social networking correctly, we wanted to invest strategically and not be held back by short-term financial limitations. In our case, raising capital corresponded with opportunity.

SM: How much did you raise? RY: We accepted $35 million last year. We raised $20 million in equity and $15 million in debt.

SM: Was Mohr Davidow the only investor? RY: Yes. Mohr Davidow was the venture investor.

SM: I know you've started the platform strategy with that $20 million. Was there a substantial infrastructure investment? RY: Not necessarily more than what we were doing prior. We're now opening up multiple data centers. Initially, we had one data center; we now have three and will probably open a fourth. That was not initially the plan, although the capital makes it easier to accomplish the inevitable sooner rather than later.

SM: Since photo sharing is such a huge piece of what you offer, doesn't that put demand on storage capabilities? I imagine 50 million users have a lot of photos. RY: Fortunately, storage costs go down exponentially.

SM: Do you limit the size of files? RY: Yes, we control the size of the photo when a user is uploading it. Beyond that we do nothing else.

SM: Where are you in terms of your platform strategy? RY: We joined Google's OpenSocial initiative in 2007 and just launched our platform in the beginning of April. It has been phenomenally successful – we see one million installs a day. We have over 400 different applications on the platform, and it has received rave reviews from developers who've been pleased with viral channels we provided them to help get their applications out to hi5 users. Additionally, a number of things we developed in OpenSocial will get rolled into the standard.

SM: You said there were 400 applications on your platform. What are those applications, and can you tell me about some of the top ones? RY: The top applications typically gravitate toward communication, interaction, and self-expression. Most of these applications are simply fun. An example of this is Super-Five. We have a feature on the site called "Fives" where you can give someone a five to say they're happy, cool, athletic, or whatever it may be. SuperFives are an expansion of that. There are some music applications which have been done really well and which allow users to select their favorite artists and place them on their profile.

Another application is the "Verb." It allows users to pick a verb and pick a friend that verb applies to. "I want to have coffee with _____," and the user picks one of their hi5 friends. It's simply a way of playing. What is interesting about platforms in general is that they enable creativity; at least that's what we have seen.

SM: Have you seen advertisers take advantage of the platforms? RY: Yes, we have. Advertisers are interested in – and this is not exclusive to applications – but advertisers are interested in identifying methods that will result in more users having a higher level of engagement with them. Applications provide a terrific way to do that. It can be accomplished through a game or some utilitarian application.

One example is a recently developed AT&T application. It's a gymnastics application, a game that has subtle advertising options weaved in, which tie into the Olympics.

SM: Did you ever see a company called Cariocas? RY: No.

SM: They're no longer around. But they had a portfolio of game theory tools including auction, reverse auction, dutch auction, and all sorts of advergames. It would be perfect for this type of application. RY: DreamWorks has also developed a widget ad on hi5 for the movie *Kung Fu Panda*.

SM: Where do you go from here as a company? RY: We continue down the path we're on right now. We see hi5 in terms of what our users want. We're trying to deliver on their desires and needs. One goal is to enable people to stay connected over a very, very long period of time, and we must provide the service that enables such communication.

Here is something I find fascinating: people who use hi5 can get a lens of what they should be seeing based on who their friends are. Today we provide that to users by showing them all the photos, blog posts, and the different Verb events our users want to have. That's a highly relevant stream of information. Down the line, we see that going beyond hi5. We envision users utilizing their relationships to help filter content on the Web as a whole. What am I reading on the Web? What newspaper article did I see that I can publish to my hi5 friends? This is how a hi5 user can consume content about issues which are relevant to them directly. Pretty soon this will move into how people consume very broad content. If you look at how much content society consumes today versus 5 to 10 years ago – just read all the blogs. That's a problem we think we can help solve.

SM: The information overload problem? Good luck! RY: There are multiple approaches. One approach is, "This is the set of information that people who matter to you are looking at, and you might want to look at this first as well." It provides a lens.

SM: Interesting. I was working for a client in Latin America last year, and I did an analysis on social networks in the region. Hi5 came up at the top continuously. It's quite amazing what you've been able to accomplish, and I wish you all the best in the future!

Validating the Market – on the Cheap

CARTS AHEAD OF HORSES

Without a market, even the greatest technologies in the world can't create business. Murli Thirumale's first startup, Net6, floundered for a time in this no-man's-land. Net6's technology for customizing computer content for mobile devices was outstanding, but companies didn't need it back in 2000. The cart had arrived before the horses.

His second startup, Ocarina Networks, is faring much better. This time around, Thirumale first identified a market – ballooning data storage – then created the requisite technologies. "I have a phrase I've coined," he says. "SDBS. It stands for sell, design, build, sell. SDBS is in contrast to designing something, building it, and then trying to sell it, which is the model most big and small tech companies follow."

Thirumale's SDBS philosophy follows that you build a proof of concept – and you can have multiple ideas leading to multiple proofs of concepts – then shop it around to customers and thought leaders. "If you do this, you'll be incredibly fast in learning, and you can pick one of your ideas with confidence," he says. "At one point in time, we had three different businesses in play, trying to figure out which would stick."

Before founding Ocarina in 2007, Thirumale asked the chief information officer of software maker Citrix what his top three problems were. Application deployment was first on his list, and the ballooning storage problem second. The Citrix CIO told Thirumale that even though the cost of media was falling, the overall cost of storage was increasing due to the overwhelming amount of data that needed storing.

With this newfound knowledge, Thirumale and his team pursued hundreds of other CIOs to discuss storage issues. Consistent feedback confirmed that the problem was not imagined, but real. And suddenly, so was Ocarina Networks. Founded with the goal of growing online storage to hold 10 times the current data, Ocarina does not look to sell new storage, but rather optimize existing storage.

Through SDBS the Ocarina team avoided wasting time on products with ambiguous value propositions. "Unlike typical startups, we spent a lot of time on validation," Thirumale says.

The result? Pure execution on an already verified premise. And, founders who have preserved a much larger stake in the company even after a significant infusion of venture capital. This time around, Murli Thirumale has ensured that the market horses are pulling Ocarina's cart with great momentum!

MURLI THIRUMALE, OCARINA

Timing is everything in venture. Launch too soon and the market may not exist; launch too late and you'll have to squeeze in among the competition.

I first worked with Murli Thirumale on his company, Net6, where it seemed he had arrived at the bazaar with a basket full of products no one wanted. However, over the next five years Murli patiently shepherded Net6 to a logical conclusion, selling it to Citrix for $50 million, then he started over. With recharged batteries. With battle-tested wisdom.

SM: Murli, let's start with your background. Tell us where you come from and a bit about what brought you to where you are today. MT: My hometown is Bangalore, the city of traffic jams! I traveled up north and went to school in Benares. From there I went right to Chicago to business school at Northwestern. After Northwestern I came out here and worked for HP for the next 15 years.

SM: What type of work did you do for HP? MT: I worked in product management, product marketing, and project management type roles. After some time I worked as GM of a couple cash cow businesses in very traditional instrumentation. I worked with technologies like atomic standards, metrology communications, and network timing.

While I was at HP, I started a couple of businesses. One was a way to synchronize base stations using GPS instead of atomic clocks.

If I'm driving down 280 like I did to get here, then I get handed off from one base station to the other. That's done today through a process of synchronizing base stations with respect to each other so the signal can be handed off. We built custom OEM GPS base station timing modules for Qualcomm, and after that it was a clean sweep of Lucent, Motorola, Samsung — about 80% of the CDMA base stations have our custom OEM, private labeled receivers in their systems.

SM: How big did that business get? MT: Business grew to about $150 million, at which point I spun it out and sold it from HP. I was still running the business, and I went with it in the sale to Symmetricom. It has now grown to become most of Symmetricom's business. I think it's a $250 million business, but a very stable business with a high market share.

SM: What is the timeline we're talking about? MT: I spun the business out of HP in 1999. Then I left Symmetricom to start Net6 in 2000.

SM: What was the idea behind Net6? MT: The original premise is very straightforward. We launched during the peak of the dotcom boom. Back then it was all about grabbing eyeballs, and the next class of eyeballs to be grabbed was mobile eyeballs. Most companies founded in that timeframe focused on building middleware. There were a few companies who wanted to offer CRM for mobile devices.

The idea we had was that expensive, custom middleware for mobile services was not the optimal solution. We found we could

make an appliance which would do all the necessary transforma-
tions required at the network level versus the middleware. We came
up with a content transformation engine appliance which would sit
on the network. It was a good concept, and we had a great OEM
deal with Cisco. It was a Cisco branded product and was launched
by Cisco. The problem was that our targets were the ISPs. Toward
the end of 2001 they all went away, so we had to reform the company around a different business.

SM: What did you decide was the repositioning strategy?
MT: The content transformation engine actually did OK. We sold
quite a bit of stuff through OEMs with Nortel, Cisco, and Avaya.
The device was IP telephone derived, so we started providing services to IP phones, but for us that was not the big business.

As we looked at the last mile of our technology, we found there
were a number of times where we were asked to encrypt data and
secure it. That became the kernel for our new product line, which
we adapted from the old code base. That product was an SSL VPN
product.

At that time we launched the SSL VPN line, and we did it
right. The SSL VPN product we built was different because instead of building it around security technology, which is how most
VPNs were built, we built it around the user experience. It was
dramatically easier to use as a VPN. It was much easier to use than
IPsec. We launched that in March of 2004, and by September of
2004 we had 100 customers.

**SM: Were you able to use the channels you'd put together,
such as Cisco and Nortel?** MT: No, it was completely different.
We weren't really able to leverage the channels, but we were able to
leverage the technology. A lot of the code base was adapted. There's
a lot of transformation required to be able to secure data.

Business grew pretty fast, and we became ankle biters for Cisco and Nortel who were selling IPsec VPNs. They became pretty

interested in us, and we got a lot of other acquisition interest as well. Through a referral from a friend, we ended up having Citrix engage with us. To make a long story short, we thought they offered the best bang for us as a company. We could have spent a lot more money ramping up channels because this was a lower cost channel play. However, as you know, that takes time – the laws of business physics. We decided the best way to grab market share was to be part of somebody who already had the channel, and Citrix had a great channel. We sold the business to them, and it ended up doing really well.

SM: What year did you sell? MT: We sold in 2005. Today the business is No. 2 in revenue behind Juniper in the SSL VPN market. When we started, we were probably the 30th company to enter that space. We were definitely not early to market; we were very late to the market. However, for the last four or five quarters, we've been first in unit revenue and second in overall revenue in the entire market.

SM: Impressive. How long did you stay there? MT: I just left last year. I was there for two years getting it ramped up.

SM: What did you do inside of Citrix? You just leveraged the channel? MT: There were two things we did really well. The first was our channel leverage, which was not self-evident. It was not a Cisco type channel, but a software application channel. Instead of selling it as a better VPN, we changed the angle.

Citrix does application delivery, so we did secure application delivery. The effect was a change in purchasing cycle by coming in through a different door. Instead of coming in the security door and beating our head against Juniper and Cisco, who had really well-entrenched buyers, we went through the application door.

The second thing is that we had a much better product.

> *We found if we got into a bake-off we won the taste test. Everybody who tried our product wanted it. All we had to do was get into the taste test.*

The way we did that was clever, and that takes us back to my first point. Instead of selling through the security buyer, we went through the application door. Our potential clients already used Citrix applications to deliver services. We let them deliver them securely. We actually changed the name from VPN to Access Gateway to access the application's security. It worked, and it worked really well.

As our business grew, Citrix gained in the security channel. There was a lot of pull afterwards. We did 45 units all of Q4, the quarter before we were sold. The next year we did a couple thousand. Now it's in the multiple thousand units.

SM: What kind of price did you get for the exit? MT: $50 million.

SM: Do you think Citrix gained more than you out of the deal? MT: Absolutely, for a variety of reasons. Aside from the pure fiscal value of the product itself, our business was very creative on many levels. Citrix had a very mature business in application virtualization. We were the first appliance company they bought. With the success they had, they bred a whole new set of technologies around selling hardware, and that built a whole new set of channels around the hardware. That increased their confidence to the point that they went out and bought NetScaler and Orbital Data. They entered the security markets and changed the positioning of the company from being an application virtualization, or thin client to company, to being an application delivery company. It was definitely a huge leverage opportunity for them.

SM: I was at your office working on a consulting engagement on 9/11. I remember we watched together as the fire raged in New York. That seemed like the worst time in history. And your entire Net6 story played out in the middle of that crazy time. MT: It did. And we started the company after the dotcom crash. The Net6 story played throughout this nuclear winter for startups. The time from 2001 through 2004 was very difficult – those were some very tough years. I'm sure you remember; it was the opposite of the irrational exuberance of the previous years. Companies funded with large amounts of money were just going out of business.

> *I remember our Series A round with some VCs, and at the time I was thinking there were two scared people in the room, I just wasn't sure who was more afraid – me or the VC. It was probably the VC – nobody knew what was going on since all the business models were turned on their heads. Unfortunately, it was a situation where having old-fashioned values did not help.*

SM: Yet you managed to raise money, you managed to sell, and you managed to grow a business to some scale in that period. What did you learn? MT: There is so much that I learned, not just from that period but from the time before as well. Ultimately the answer is: find the real opportunity.

SM: Yet your first opportunity did not click; you had to adjust. MT: It was a real opportunity, but it went away. There is no point pursuing something when the opportunity disappears. It's a myth that startups create markets; startups take advantage of opportunities. Fundamentally, you have to start with an opportunity.

SM: At minimum you have to start with a hypothesis, then correct course as you go along. MT: Start with a hypothesis and then verify it as quickly as possible. One of the things I have learned over time, and Net6 is a great example because we did three different businesses in mobility, IP telephony, and SSL VPN, is that you don't rationalize your strategy. I have a phrase I have coined: SDBS. It stands for sell, design, build, sell.

> *SDBS is in contrast to designing something, building it, and then trying to sell it, which is the model most big and small tech companies follow. A lot of startups are based on a hypothesis – they build something and start interacting with customers, but they never verify it. What they are doing is rationalizing the hypothesis rather than evaluating and verifying it.*

SDBS is a philosophy where essentially you build a proof of concept, and you can have multiple ideas, then you go shop your concept to two sets of constituencies – customers and thought leaders. If you do this, you'll be incredibly fast in learning, and you can pick one of your ideas with confidence. At one point in time we had three different businesses in play, trying to figure out which would stick. What stuck was SSL VPN.

SM: But you couldn't have guessed that sitting in your office; you had to get into the game, start playing with the market. MT: There has to be traction with the world. The beauty is that once you do SDBS, if you have something people want, the rest is easy. It's easy in the sense that when you work hard and execute well, you can get revenue. You are not just paddling really hard to get nowhere, which is what happens in most of these things. I have used SDBS many times. We used it to start Ocarina, too.

SM: Let's talk about Ocarina. What was the genesis? MT: Once I knew Citrix was doing well, I was ready to turn it over to somebody else. I asked the CIO of Citrix what his top three problems were. Application deployment was first on his list. As far as I'm concerned, anybody doing a big Oracle or SAP deployment will have that as their number one problem because you can get fired if it doesn't go well. The incredible storage problem was second on his list.

With that in mind, we did the SDBS model again. We SDBS'd the Ocarina idea with two other ideas in completely separate realms. One was an e-business, a Web 2.0 business, and the other was an image recognition technology. The reason we picked Ocarina was that this was where customers consistently came back and said they had a huge pain point around.

SM: Explain the pain point a bit more. MT: The pain point is very straightforward. We were talking about Web 2.0 earlier. The world has changed, and businesses are hit with it all the time. There is so much rich media out there in the form of images, video, office documents, etc. All of these things are accumulating, and one of the side effects is that you need lots of room to store it. The typical home user's storage has gone up dramatically in the past years, so just multiply that a thousand fold and you're at the enterprise level. Then imagine the challenge for market leaders. Basically, storage skyrockets. Even though the cost of media is falling, the overall cost of storage is increasing. And the amount to be stored overwhelms everything else.

The value proposition we present is that we will go in and optimize your online storage, which is the storage you use on a regular basis, and allow you to store up to 10 times more on the storage devices you already have. We do this by installing an Ocarina appliance on your existing storage network. We are not a storage vendor. We are not asking you to buy storage from us. We simply make whatever storage you already have much more efficient.

SM: Is it like a network-level defragmenter, conceptually? MT: In a sense that's one of the things we do. Defragging is absolutely one of the strategies. We come in, install the appliance, and literally the next day we will have crawled through five terabytes and freed up 70–80% of the space. We deliver three terabytes of additional storage space per day, which you can put to use immediately.

SM: It's a simple idea. MT: Very simple!

SM: I like that. MT: Everybody gets it, and everybody wants it. The nice thing is that in one sense it's not new. There are people who have done this for different parts of data. They've done this on the Wide Area Network. As data is sent from a branch to a central office, you just reduce it so you use less bandwidth.

SM: True, but you are solving a very different problem. MT: Exactly. The technologies utilized for data in motion and data in rest are very different.

SM: You're not alone in the market, but I think you're going after a niche which has been ignored somewhat. MT: Yes. We mentioned earlier the WAN concepts, where people are compressing the data because of the narrow pipes. Companies have done it for backup solutions as well. That's a huge subcategory in this space as well. With backups there are a lot of duplicates. From one week to the next 90% of the data is the same. It's pretty straightforward that you only need one instance of a file stored as long as it can be referenced by multiple storage backup restoration indexes.

I like our niche because we have the same value propositions, but it's for online storage, which is more expensive. The challenge, of course, is that online storage does not have nearly as many duplicate files as the backup category. Hardly any of the files we deal with are duplicate files.

SM: Who are the primary clients you sell to? Do you focus on datacenter vendors? MT: It's not limited to a datacenter, nor is it intended only for large enterprises. The people who have the biggest problems are Internet media, and they're our first target market. We're pretty much in evaluation in all the big photo shops. We're also talking with all the e-mail companies, the social networks, and a lot of the managed service providers who do hosting. Thus Internet media is one major group for us. Then there are all the media and entertainment guys like Fox Media and the animation and video companies. They comprise a second major group for us. Finally, you have another category consisting of oil and gas companies who do a lot of simulation and seismic data.

SM: You're already at a stage where you're selling to all of these people? MT: We're just starting with Internet media, and oil and gas has just started.

SM: How big is your sales force? MT: When I say we just started, it is very literal – we launched last week! We'll be shipping this month. We're undergoing evaluations in six places right now.

SM: This is a great story. I like that it's highly defined technology with an obvious market need. Who is the technologist behind this? MT: We have a bunch of different types of people. The first are high-speed network proxy folks. That's in line with the Net6 group. Then we have some storage people, because there's a lot of file system awareness. The third category are the compression experts. Those are guys whose heads bulge in strange places, and they have three PhDs apiece, from all over the world. Those are the three extremes of the types of people we hire.

SM: When you started the company, you identified the problem. After that what was the evolution of building the company? MT: Let's talk about the customer validation part because that was the beginning. We built a proof of concept, and while we were building it, we went out and hired a third-party storage analyst firm to conduct a market evaluation for us. The reason we did that was because we didn't want to taint the data with our own excitement and passion. We wanted as objective an evaluation as possible. When the analysts came back and said it was a great market, we weren't surprised. Since we had concurrently been building a proof of concept, we were already well on our way. In summary, the first year we built the algorithms and validated the market. Unlike typical startups, we spent a lot of time on validation. It has paid off in spades. All the money we're now investing is in the right place, and we don't need course correction.

> *A lot of times the first 6, 7, or even 10 months of a startup you're doing the "Moses' 40 years in the wilderness" game. Our value proposition has not changed once. We've stayed true to course.*

SM: It's straightforward execution. MT: And we've been very focused on that execution. Only after we built the proof of concept and tried it out with a couple of customers, and had results which showed we were getting huge amounts of optimization, did we then decide to go raise funds.

SM: You seeded the company yourself and hired a bunch of algorithm people for the prototype? MT: Correct. I would much rather do it this way every time.

SM: If you can afford to, this is the ideal way. This is where being a serial entrepreneur pays off because you know what to do. MT: Everything, like raising money, was easier this time around. We had a huge amount of interest this time, so we were able to pick and choose who we wanted. I would rather raise money from customers than VCs, but sometimes you have to use VCs.

SM: What were the deciding factors on what VCs you chose? MT: There were two things. We went for the right brand and the right people, not in any particular order. We got some great guys on the board, people-wise. They have a lot of experience.

SM: Who's on the board? MT: Peter Bell from Highland Capital. Peter was the CEO of Storage Networks, and he knows everybody in storage. He's a great guy. We also have Matt Murphy of Kleiner Perkins. He's been very helpful. We did a lot of diligence with our VCs, and I've been very impressed with Kleiner. I did not expect it. There are always people with a lot of aura, so you never know. We also have B. V. Jagadeesh on the board as an independent. He's a very seasoned guy and very supportive.

SM: Are your sales initially going to be direct? MT: Initially, yes. I really believe that's the only way to do it initially, and probably the best way overall. I will mention that we've had a lot of partner interest, so I'm not throwing that option out the door. If you think about it, there is a big ecosystem in storage. From our perspective at Ocarina the value proposition and the product are really, really simple and straightforward. It lends itself well to a channel play.

SM: That is true. Salespeople are not going to have any problem grasping the value proposition. MT: Not only that, but we learned a lot about channel plays from our Net6 SSL and VPN experience. Ease of deployment and ease of installation make a huge difference. Plus, if we have the right channels, we can once again experience customer pull versus channel push. I always prefer to deal with customer pull.

SM: A simple message really helps a lot as well. MT: Agreed, and there are three reasons why, although we're not there yet.

First, if you look at it, we really have a horizontal problem. Anybody with more than 200 terabytes, with storage requirements growing more than 20% a year, is a candidate for Ocarina. If their storage demands are not growing, it does not work for us. For potential clients the ROI is literally three or four months. The beauty of it is there's a very simple event – likely already planned – which will help our clients purchase an Ocarina appliance: their next storage purchase. They can either purchase an Ocarina, or they can buy more storage. We expect people will use the budget they were going to buy storage with and use it instead to buy an Ocarina. If they spend just a bit more on their next quarterly purchase, they will spend less forever.

Second, there's a simple value proposition. And finally, it's a simple installation, not a complex professional services type of play.

SM: Congratulations. It's a fine story and a great opportunity.

MANOJ SAXENA, WEBIFY

Successful in his first go at entrepreneurship with Exterprise, Manoj felt the pressing need to test himself: "Was I lucky, or was I good?"

With the success of Webify, his second venture, Manoj once and for all set those doubts to rest.

Manoj presents an astute discourse on innovation and early product idea validation, and reconciles the perspective presented by Murli Thirumale in the earlier story with that of the legendary Steve Jobs.

SM: Where did you grow up, Manoj? MS: I grew up in India. A city called Hyderabad most of my life, then we were down in Bombay.

SM: What was your family like? Were you exposed early on to entrepreneurship? MS: Not a whole lot. My father's generation was the first generation that had to work for a living. They were mostly into professional careers. There were a couple uncles who'd tried their hand at some manufacturing businesses that actually bombed. In general it was not something that was encouraged or seen as an exciting career. I was mostly encouraged to be an engineer or doctor. Most of my entrepreneurial ambitions, I think, grew out of my time and experience in Pilani and then after I moved to the US.

SM: So, what was going on in Pilani when you were there? MS: Actually it's kind of funny. My girlfriend at that time – now my wife – and I went to school there together. Pilani is a campus about 100 miles away from any large city, and I used to take her out for dates. But she never allowed me to pay for her food. She would say, "It's your parents' money and my parents' money; we're going dutch." It used to annoy the hell out of me. I figured I've got to make my own money. So, staying on the campus [far from the city], I took up the opportunity to sell pictures at a very heavy premium to freshmen.

SM: Really? MS: Yes, I arranged for a photographer who was about 20 miles away and paid some guys, and so it was mostly driven by more of a need to...

SM: Impress your girlfriend! MS: Exactly, exactly.

SM: OK, and then after Pilani – you came to the US? MS: I worked in India for a couple of years with a company called ITC. I went up to the management training program and spent a couple of years there. Then I came to the US in 1988 to go to Michigan State in East Lansing, and right after that I was hired by 3M. That was 1990. I joined 3M and stayed with them for eight years, running a business unit for them in telecom.

In 1998, this is before the boom time of the Internet, a couple of things happened. I started seeing the whole Internet potential. Then my second daughter was born, and I had a strong desire to build.

Professionally, I was doing very well at 3M.

> *In eight years, I had seven promotions, and stuff like that. So I couldn't complain, but what I wanted to do professionally was build something that leaves a legacy behind.*

At one level I saw the children coming up and said to myself that the 3M handcuffs were only going to get golden, and those golden handcuffs would only get diamond studded. I said this is the time to quit. So I took 13 credit cards with $200,000 of credit, quit 3M, and started my first company.

SM: What was that like psychologically – was it scary?
MS: It was downright scary. It took almost four to five times more courage than I thought it would take. I had people's payroll on my shoulders and this $200,000 in credit cards – but I was paying everyone a check. In a strange way it was also a strong motivator. The first issue I had to get over was the psychological or social issue of people back home in India thinking I'm an idiot for having left a fast-growing career in 3M to start something new. So it was the social part that was the first kind of pressure.

Then the other one after that was that I had six employees within three or four months. I formed some projects, and it was the pressure of meeting payroll and making sure that these guys were taken care of. Those were the more difficult times.

> *SM: How did your wife react to your quitting 3M?*
> *MS: Well, I call my wife my first venture capitalist.*

One of the things I did was to create an Excel sheet analysis of what happens if everything goes to hell with this $200,000 credit thing. I showed her that we would basically have to sell our house and move to a condo. But in about two and a half years we could pay the debt off. The second thing was what I called a "get out of jail card." I told her that when starting a new company the *honey-do-this list* on the weekends – I wouldn't be able to do much about it for the next two years and she shouldn't get too upset. I asked for those two things, and she completely backed me.

SM: Did she have a job, or was there another source of income? MS: No, she had a job. She was working at IBM as an IT architect. She had gone part-time as well because we wanted her to take care of our children. I didn't want her to have to go back to work just because of my entrepreneur thing, so we went from basically 200 units of income to 50 units of income. But, you know she supported me to the hilt. That's why I call her my first VC.

SM: What was your first company? MS: It was basically a business collaboration platform called Exterprise. We started in June of 1998 and sold it in March of 2001. We grew pretty rapidly from five initial employees to over 240 people within 18 months. We sold it for $114 million to Commerce One. We'd raised about $28 million in cash from very good VC funds like Morgan Stanley, Dell, and Austin Ventures.

SM: How did those connections happen? MS: When I first started, I was told I had to have very good lawyers and accountants. So I went to the best legal firm in Austin, Wilson Sonsini. I talked to their lawyers and basically told them I couldn't pay them their $400-to $500-an-hour-bill, but what I could do was buy them lunch at any place of their choice and get advice over lunch, and eventually, if I got funded, they would become my lawyers. I didn't want to spend the $200,000 credit card capital on $400-an-hour lawyer fees. Through them I got introductions to people within town.

SM: Why did you pick Austin? MS: I moved down with 3M for a business unit, 3M Telecom, here in Austin.

SM: So Austin was already your home base by then. MS: Out of the eight years I was with 3M, I was five years in St. Paul, then they moved me down to Austin in 1995 to run a portion of the telecom business.

SM: So Wilson Sonsini put you in contact with some of their VC contacts? MS: Right. And another executive from Synoptics, Shelby Carter – I got to know him, and he wanted to get on board. At that time Shelby had the choice of running the campaign finance for President Bush, or being the non-executive chairman for my company. He was convinced and impressed enough to come in and join us as an investor.

SM: So that was your angel investment, from Shelby? And how much was that? MS: About $200,000.

SM: And how far did that take you? MS: If I remember right, we raised our first venture funding in February of 1999, so seven months.

SM: And that got you to a prototype, or customers? MS: Yeah, it got me the first couple customers, and it also got us to another version of the first prototype.

SM: And then you received your first funding? Any other highlights during that period of building Exterprise? MS: Yeah, one of the things that stood out was the quality of customers we were able to get. It was 1998 when we started and 1999 when this whole thing started picking up. We had a pretty impressive customer list: Bell Canada, John Deere, Dell, and companies like that.

> *One of the highlights was when Michael Dell stood up in a conference and demonstrated the Exterprise product as the way Dell was going to do e-commerce in the future.*

I look back at that as something significant. Then again, growing from 5 people to 240 in 18 months, that was quite a rush. Also, opening our offices in the UK and Southeast Asia. I think those were all pretty good memories.

SM: How did you get into Dell? MS: Dell, again, was one of the first things we had done. Michael Dell had his own personal investment arm called MSD Capital. They had looked into funding us, and then they asked for some terms. I walked away from them because they wanted terms that didn't work. About eight months after turning that money down, Dell Ventures came to us. They'd heard of Exterprise from other people as a high-growth company, and they came in to talk to us and invested in us. Following that we took that opportunity to go and sell our product to Dell.

SM: In mid- to late 2000 the Internet market started to crash. How did it go for your company? MS: In late 2000 it didn't crash for us; we had about four other offers for acquisitions in the meantime. I continued to want to build this into a large company, so we turned them all down. Commerce One had reached out to us in July of 2000 and had given us about a $110 million offer, and I said no to them.

SM: What was the revenue at this point? MS: Revenue was about $18 million.

SM: So 18 months, $18 million. A huge ramp. MS: Actually, in 2000 we did about $18 million in bookings, not revenues. Revenues would probably be about $12 million.

SM: Still a very good run. MS: On the other side, one of the things that we found was, as we started getting into Q4 of 2000, the sales cycle changed. In December of 2000 we had a $15 million pipeline, and we were expecting to close $7–$8 million of that. Suddenly, in December, I started taking a lot of phone calls from CFOs. We're talking about them writing a million- or two-million-dollar check, and with all of these dotcoms failing they began asking, "How do I know you guys will be around?"

At that time we were really going gangbusters, so I realized this was not an issue about my product or my people, it was just an issue of customer confidence. So, I called back Mark Hoffman, CEO of Commerce One, and told him if he was still interested in discussing the purchase, we should have dinner and talk about it.

Over dinner he said he'd give the same terms he was going to give back in July. But by that time we had even more business, had gotten a couple more accounts. The fact that Hoffman approached it with a lot of professionalism, I basically came back to the board and said, "Let's take this offer and sell the company."

SM: You've now sold the company at the end of 2000 – are you staying on as an executive at Commerce One? MS: We sold it in early 2001. I was staying on to build an enterprise strategy for them. All of their products and sales were in exchanges; they didn't have any enterprise sales. So I decided to stay on with them to build out a vertical enterprise strategy solution. Unfortunately, I was with them for over a year when I could have left the very next day.

First I decided to stay back six months and make sure my team was well integrated in the right jobs, the right positions and all. Within the six month period the market had really gotten worse. We're talking about the middle of 2001. Commerce One's revenues really started falling off a cliff. I didn't feel at that time I should be jumping ship, so I stayed on further.

Commerce One had hired another president, Dennis Jones. I had some pretty aggressive proposals that I made to Mark Hoffman, one of which was to take a large portion of engineering and move it offshore. I explored a couple companies in India for him. For some reason Dennis and I couldn't see eye to eye on some of those strategies, so I stayed long enough to do the sales launch, then left to found Webify.

SM: Were you still based in Austin, or did you move to the Valley? MS: No, I was commuting to the Valley three to four days a week. In the meantime my team had taken on more and more prominent roles; they were really the stars in Commerce One. When I left, Hoffman wanted me to give him my word that I wouldn't go after their employees, so I didn't hire a single technical guy. I built Webify with an entirely new group of engineers.

SM: In the case of Webify, you were funding it with your own money, right?

MS: *Right, the first million bucks, I wrote those checks myself.*

The interesting part with Webify was I started it in March 2002 and had the hardest time finding pilot customers. This was in the middle of the nuclear winter of IT. No one wanted to talk to you. The last person who did that lost their job trying new stuff. So one of the things I did was I went out and bought the controlling interest in a company out of India that had 50-odd customers, many multinational customers. I sent my VP of engineering over there; I went there for a month and started selling to companies like Johnson & Johnson, Cadbury, and Pfizer. Johnson & Johnson is still running our product.

My goal was to get brand name customers in India, then come back to the US. We were doing this in India because no US customer would talk to us. My conviction was that there were still very large and hairy problems to be solved. As long as those problems are there, the market phenomenon is a temporary one. So, as I said, there is no bear market for good ideas.

SM: I guess it depends on whether companies can survive a downturn. MS: That's right.

> *That's exactly why my mantra used to be "Take a little money, and build a lot of value."*

So we did that, and interestingly enough as we were doing that, even though customers were hard to get, money was not difficult to get. We had a $6 million investment offer in Webify, but we didn't need it and actually turned it down. If I took too much money and the market didn't go right, I would have lost the whole company. Instead of raising $6 million, we raised $750,000 in two batches while validating the market and building enough of a pipeline.

We did about $1.1 million the first year and $5.5 million the next, then $13 million the third year. We're on target this year, but I can't give you the number because IBM has put all kinds of restraints on them.

SM: And you were already acquired in 2006. And that number is not public either, correct? MS: It's not public, but it's in the neighborhood of the first company's acquisition. There's a good multiple with a great return.

SM: It's interesting what you said earlier: you were offered $6 million and turned it down to take only $750,000, giving you room to validate the market. That's a very wise decision that less sophisticated entrepreneurs would not make. MS: Exactly, because we learned and I saw this in 2000 and 2001 when I used to meet other CEOs among entrepreneurs. It was almost a badge of merit, how much money you raised. Which is really quite the opposite of how entrepreneurs should look at it. It's true, it's a bit counterintuitive.

> *If you raise a lot of money, you're leveraging the hell out of yourself. And you probably have a lot of people wanting to grab the steering wheel if things don't go right.*

SM: What is your own personal core competency? Is it engineering, is it sales, marketing? MS: I would say that it's a combination of product management and sales. My core competency is being able to study a market and identify some deep trends, being able to anticipate the trend and start building products and technologies to intersect the trend. The second core competency, without being boastful, is having the ability to identify, hire, and recruit world-class talent.

SM: How do you think you developed the former skill set? MS: I think a big part of it was the time I spent at 3M. They have this program where they hire three or four MBAs every year from different business schools around the country. They put you through a boot camp where you work with different general managers and vice presidents on a variety of problems dealing with new product launches, marketing, divestures, or acquisitions. Typically people do two or three projects there. I think my average workload was seven projects over the three years I was there. I used to call it the 3M buffet table, because 3M had something like 45 different business units. I think this whole process of staying close to the customer, observing and anticipating the user's needs, and going and building a product based on that is something where at 3M I really got to hone my skills.

SM: Do you normally envision a product a customer is likely to need? Or do you listen to customers, then come up with your ideas? MS: I think it's a combination of both – a combination of selecting technologies, then applying them. A lot of it is anticipation of some technologies on the horizon that could solve really deep problems a customer could have.

SM: The reason I'm drilling this is that if you listen to Steve Jobs, the customer can never tell you what product they want because they have no idea what's possible. MS: Absolutely, absolutely. When I was in 3M, I did some work with Erick Jaun Hipple at MIT on this whole area called Lead User Innovation. The concept there is exactly what you said, that if you ask a customer you'll never get the right answer. However, there is a very small minority of customers out there called Lead Users, according to this framework that Juan Hipple has worked out.

> *A Lead User is typically a person who has such a strong need or pain that they go out and build something on their own to solve the pain.*

The goal of the process is to be able to identify those Lead Users, identify how they're solving their problem, and bring it back and commercialize the product for mass markets.

SM: How do you identify Lead Users? MS: That is a whole discipline. For example in Webify, which I did in early 2002, I went and spent six months at Wells Fargo with Steve Ellis, who's a good friend and a VP at Wells Fargo. I used to just go and spend time there and talk to their architects to try to really understand what their issues were with their business in general. There were some very big problems that were still there. E-business technologies of 2002 were not solving them.

SM: What were some of the nuggets from your Wells Fargo discussions? MS: Actually, the first Wells Fargo market we thought we would go after was a failure. I had to recalibrate the strategy to apply it to another market. The same technology, but a different market.

In the case of Exterprise I started applying the technology to automated processes to diagnose problems for telecom networks.

Though this first application area didn't pan out, the same technology ended up being applicable in e-commerce.

The same thing with Webify. Even though it was under different architectures, we thought we would go after banking with this emerging technology called Service Oriented Architecture (SOA). I realized that SOA had a lot of limitations with performance and security, which would not make it a good candidate for banking. Therefore, we applied it to healthcare, insurance, and other verticals.

SM: Where are you now in your frame of mind? You're at IBM obviously, but are you going to stay at IBM? MS: Well, I am at IBM right now. I'm still running the Webify business unit. What has been very satisfying for me to see is the impact we're having on transforming both IBM's Global Services and their software group. This is IBM's first joint acquisition between their software group and Global Services.

> *I want to build, and I want to make sure my products and technologies are going to make an impact on thousands, if not tens of thousands, of customers globally.*

IBM gives me a global platform to complete the journey and vision I had of leaving a personal legacy behind – something that didn't happen with Commerce One. I'm staying on for a couple of years to make sure that this product, which IBM has now launched as WebSphere Fabric, is successful. I went to China to open the China center, the ribbon-cutting ceremony and all. Sitting back and watching the proceedings, you know, when I saw the word "IBM" written next to "Fabric" in Chinese, it was a very proud moment. I think I'm emotionally committed to making sure this product sticks and becomes the crown jewel of IBM's SOA portfolio so that I can tell my grandchildren about this stuff.

SM: Assuming your grandchildren will care! MS: They may not, but at least they'll hear it!

SM: There's actually a slightly tongue-in-cheek part to that comment: by the time we have grandchildren, they'll probably take all of this for granted. Just like we take the telephone for granted. MS: They'll tell us we're so old. I like to say that when you're done and gone, all you leave behind is your children and what Google says about you.

SM: Before Google there was nothing actually. No epitaph, so to speak. MS: Exactly, so I would like Google to have some cool things to say in a small way. We will be able to move the needle forward in certain areas.

SM: And what are you doing with your wealth? Are you investing in new companies? Are you doing philanthropy? What's the destiny of the wealth you've created? MS: Well, a couple of things. First, I'm contributing to the economy right now by spending. I'm doing my part from the consumer's point of view. But more importantly, 90% of my stock from the two companies will not go to my children. We have a foundation in place called the Saxena Foundation. We have quite a number of initiatives. There are three or four initiatives we're doing in India, some in America. We have a classroom named [after the foundation] at Michigan State. Now there's a chair back in Pilani. In the foundation we're going to put a provision in place that any member of our family out of America or India, if they are able to get into any of the Ivy League schools, the foundation will pay for four years of their education.

On a personal level, you know after the Commerce One deal I tried to retire and ended up almost getting a divorce because I was bouncing off the walls. My wife suggested to me gently that I should go start another company.

SM: So that's not going to happen again? MS: I don't think so. I've got a strong desire for what I call brain candy.

SM: Any overriding, unrealized visions or dreams at this point? MS: That's a great question. I feel incredibly blessed and grateful for all of the opportunities and breaks that have come about. I think the one thing would be to be a better human being. That sounds very philosophical, but I think to be a more rounded human being would be my unrealized dream. Being a more patient person, because patience is not my virtue. Being a better family person with a balance of home and family life. Some stuff like that.

SM: You're only 41; you have a lot of time left. MS: I've gone to places for a month where you don't talk and you meditate for four hours a day and all of that. It was one of the most insightful and difficult things I've ever done in my life. It did help a lot. It's apparently the same concept that Buddha went through for three years before he obtained enlightenment.

> *The whole deal is that for 10 days you still your mind and turn it inward. The concept is that you are who you are because of the knowledge from the entirety of your life, the cravings and aversions – your knots.*

When you still your mind and open up those knots, you go back and things happen. I went back to when I was four or five years old, as well as when I was seven. I began to notice things that my father said to me when I brought home report cards that made me so driven.

SM: Is it a facilitated process, or independent? MS: It's a facilitated process. It's done out of four centers in the US and some 50 centers around the world. Every two hours they talk to you for five minutes. They tell you how to meditate, and then they go away. You do it in a room where 10 or 15 other people are sitting as well. There's no chanting or anything; it's just quiet, stilling your mind. You don't talk. There are two meals a day. You do it for 10 days.

There are so many things I don't know. One thing I am pretty confident about is that this is my last startup. The next thing will probably be a private equity setup where you get together a $100 million or so and buy up a few companies. Restructure them, recalibrate them, make them into a global enterprise, and work it globally. Flip it. That sort of thing.

SM: Tired of starting from scratch? MS: Yes, it is a different experience. One of the reasons I did Webify was to answer a question about my first company: was I good, or was I lucky? My wife says I'm just a masochist. My sense was that any idiot could have done it had you given them $18 million in 1998.

SM: You had something to prove to yourself. MS: That's a big portion of it. Proving to myself that it was not just a fluke. So I think the two areas I'm going to do something in are first, social entrepreneurship, where 70% is still about making money and 30% is about doing good. I have this personal motto of "doing well by doing good." The second thing would be a private equity deal on a larger scale, because it's a different type of challenge. It's just that I want to test myself in different areas. It's all about learning and growing. Ready for climbing new mountains, that kind of thing.

SM: Well, thank you for sharing your journey. And good luck with those future mountains.

RESURRECTING
THE DEAD

Silicon Lazarus

If you've been around long enough, you've heard this narrative before: The market is grinding to a halt, the IPO window is shut, and only a few brave souls dare venture out into the turbulent seas. The mergers and acquisitions market is adrift as well; public companies are under stock price pressure; further down the value chain, the startups – especially the venture-funded ones – are stuck in an exit-starved no-man's-land.

You can sit around, depressed, or as some technology startup veterans will tell you, you can pick up great technologies at rock-bottom prices and build businesses out of them. Big businesses.

Lars Dalgaard, chief executive of SuccessFactors, based in San Mateo, California, a maker of talent management software, could offer you a blueprint. In the dotcom carnage of 2001, Dalgaard, fresh out of business school, bought several companies – among them, eAlity. Believe it or not, he bought two of these Web-based software companies at an auction in Redwood City, California. "I don't remember how old I was, maybe 31, and I was taking on $3.2 million in debt to own this company," Dalgaard recounts. "I figured I would do whatever I could to build it up."

And what did all this debt get him? A big, scalable, on-demand platform built by three Chinese supercomputing geniuses stationed in the supercomputing labs of the University of California, Berkeley. "They had built this twice already. Talk about pioneering On Demand – they were way before anyone else," Dalgaard says. "These guys had built an outstanding, one-code, scalable supercomputing platform, but they didn't have a CEO."

They also did not have much of a product vision, which Dalgaard brought with him. He wanted to build a company that developed Web-based software to manage human resources functions.

Foundation Capital had invested in eAlity early on, so the natural bridge was already in place for Dalgaard to seek funding. But Foundation turned him down – he wasn't a Silicon Valley guy. Originally from Denmark, Dalgaard had spent most of his career at Unilever in Europe. Dalgaard, however, caught the ear of the legendary David Strohm of Greylock, who remained skeptical at first. "He just sat there and looked at me like, 'Who the hell are you, and what do you know about anything?'" Dalgaard says. But Strohm was involved in one of the other companies Dalgaard had bought at auction, and Dalgaard's passion turned infectious.

"I'll give you a million," Strohm told Dalgaard, "and you see what you can do with it. That's it. You're never going to get anything more if you don't do something incredible with it."

Dalgaard took eAlity and turned it into SuccessFactors. But the timing wasn't good; the company launched its first product three days after the September 11th attacks.

But Dalgaard made SuccessFactors cash flow positive soon after, and from there on funding was easy to come by. Dalgaard also became an adept fundraiser, raising $45 million over multiple rounds from Greylock, TPG, Emergence Capital, Eric Dunn at Cardinal Venture Partners, and others between 2003 and 2007. A year after going public in 2007, the company currently boasts a market cap of over $650 million. In July of 2008, SuccessFactors crossed four million users and expects to generate $108 million in revenues by year's end.

So why do I bring up Dalgaard and SuccessFactors now? The current market, in a far greater abyss than it was between 2000 and 2003, is becoming increasingly difficult to navigate. But it's the kind of market that entrepreneurs with strong leadership skills, business acumen, and turnaround expertise can also play to their advantage.

Our valley of geeks has always built wonderful, rocket-science technology, often without any idea what problems the technology would eventually solve. Other times, these visionaries have built technology with an idea of what problem to solve, but set out with a flawed market strategy. From sophisticated artificial intelligence algorithms to chip testing at 45 nanometers, these engineers' achievements are always humbling. But they need business savvy to make and sell products.

Venture capitalists have plowed millions into such ventures, and many are now approaching a breaking point. Either the VCs want an exit, or the founders – after years of muscling their companies forward – are exhausted. These ventures are starved for new leadership to rejuvenate them or, in some cases, resuscitate them.

LARS DALGAARD, SUCCESSFACTORS

Think you need to have Silicon Valley DNA to become a successful technology entrepreneur? Lars Dalgaard proves it ain't so. Lars is the CEO of SuccessFactors, a SaaS company which went public in 2007 with explosive energy.

Dalgaard's personal success factors are rooted in that same inextinguishable energy that powers his adventures. Call it passion, call it arrogance, call it a desire for excellence – his level of intensity rarely leaves you indifferent.

SM: Lars, I want to start with your personal background – tell me who you are. LD: You don't have that much time! I was born in Denmark – I have a Danish passport. I lived in Denmark until I was 18, with a brief stint in England from 13 to 16.

SM: Did you come to the US when you were 18? LD: I wasn't smart enough to get a scholarship to the American schools, and I didn't have any money to afford it on my own. Out of undergraduate I started working for Novartis, a pharmaceutical company. They had 70,000 employees. I went to work for them in Switzerland, which was a very interesting experience. I also worked for them in New York for a while before returning to Switzerland. It was a very global experience in a very short time.

SM: What were your functional areas of work? LD: Novartis has a program where they select two people every year who they think have the potential to become managers of their core business areas. They take them very young – I was the youngest by about 10 years, and somehow I got in – and they train you.

They made me a corporate controller first, which meant I had to learn all of the accounting bugs. Pharmaceutical companies make a lot of money, particularly the top three which Novartis was at the time, so they are very concerned about how they control the cash. They teach you a lot about the inner workings of the businesses.

It's funny because I haven't thought about that in some 15 years, but that is one of the reasons I drive my company with so many metrics – that was how they did it. Their process evolved over many years. They've gone down to a level where they want each pharmaceutical pill to cost nothing so they can spend billions in research and development and have a high profit, which of course they do.

After that they send you to the US, as a training ground. The entire program is like a two-year boot camp where they drop you in and see if you survive. It's that principle the whole way through. You're put in sales school, then sent to the field to be a sales rep. In my case I was a foreigner, and I ended up selling cardiology products to cardiologists in New Jersey in the biggest hospitals.

> *Overall, it was a very simple process – if you survive, you are one of us; if you don't, then find another job.*

When you were done being a sales rep, they sent you to the head office to become a product manager where you learned advertising and media. After you make it through that, they send you back to the head office for more advertising and brainwashing. You're then supposed to be sent out into operations. By that time, however, I was really bored.

SM: How many years were you with Novartis? LD: I think it was two and half or three years.

SM: So you moved through all of those functions in just two and a half years? LD: That's how they do it once you're in that group they want to promote.

SM: That is great – a crash course in business! LD: I'm the luckiest person in the world. It is absolutely fabulous. I am very, very blessed with that.

SM: What years are we talking? LD: That was 1991, 1992, and 1993.

SM: Right before the Internet struck. LD: That's right! And I was stuck over in Switzerland somewhere skiing.

SM: What happened after you left Novartis? LD: This all ties into how I ended up starting my company. I remember being headhunted by Unilever, a big company with 320,000 employees and $60 billion in sales at the time. I remember walking into the global VP of HR at Novartis and telling him, "Hey, you probably don't care, but I'm going to join Unilever, and I'm leaving today."

He exploded, started saying, "Hold on, hold on!" I swear to God, he got this key out of his pocket that was on a little string, and he went over and opened a closet and pulled out this huge three-ring binder, skimmed through it, and pulled out all these org charts. "See, here you are," he said. "You're going to be running Portugal in two years!"

I was standing there – "What? What are you talking about?" He came back and said, "Well, that's not the only one. I have you in Germany, but that's a lower job. I also have you–" and he started going through all these pages. I was shocked; I was standing there thinking, "This is how they manage careers?"

SM: What job were you going to be taking at Unilever? LD: I was going to run a product globally, which was very exciting. I had just gotten into Harvard Business School, and I turned it down because I couldn't imagine anything more exciting. At the time globalization was what everybody was talking about.

SM: You left to run a product globally, but what happened after that? How long did you stay? LD: I was supposed to stay in that job for four or five years, but I got promoted a year later because the product had become very successful. It became a $200 million product. I was lucky because I was 26, and they sent me to Germany to run a company of 60 people. That is extremely lucky to run a company at such a young age. It was a great learning experience for me because they had already put a lot of structures in place.

SM: Was that a subsidiary of Unilever? LD: Yes, it was. They had 13 subsidiaries at the time, and each had hundreds of little companies inside.

> *I remember listening to the CEO's speech at a conference, and somebody asked how many companies they acquired a month. He said it was at least one or two before the CFO pulled him over to tell him it was 13 a month.*

SM: Did they integrate them, or let them run under a general manager? LD: Sometimes when they were big they integrated them. However, when they were small pockets, they just let GMs run the company. That was one of the biggest learning experiences of my life. That was the first time I experienced the power of Web technology.

We were doing something as boring as cleaning Coca-Cola factories. I don't know if you can imagine that mammoth. But you can feel comfortable opening and drinking that product because it's made in such a sterile environment. That's the product we delivered, but here's the interesting thing: in Germany where I lived, there were 22 Coke plants, but we distributed from one central location. What we created was what the CEO was really worried about, because if he did not have hygiene, it was game over. Remember when there were rats in some Wendy's in New York? That's what it was like for these guys – they would *die* without hygiene.

We created the ability for him to sit in his home, on his laptop, and see what was going on in all of his factories. I will never forget his face when I gave him that laptop. His eyes freaked out, and I told myself right there that I was going to do something in technology. The guy was paralyzed! "I can control all of my Coke factories from my home?" he said. He could not stop talking about it. That was the second place where I learned the value of technology.

SM: How long did you stay in that job at Unilever? LD: I moved back to the head office after a year, which was unfortunate because I really liked that job. They moved me back because we bought our biggest competitor, and they asked me if I could travel around the biggest countries and understand whom we should keep and whom we should fire, and then merge the two companies into one.

After that I went to Denmark, still for Unilever. We bought a company there, and I ran that acquisition. I then began managing that company, and shortly afterwards we bought five other companies, and I had to put them together as well.

SM: What kind of companies were you buying in Denmark? Did any of them have anything to do with technology?
LD: One had kitchen cleaning products – nothing at all to do with technology. I did build technology products in my own little world for my groups.

For instance, I would come in and sit down with my team, who were all 20 years older than me, and ask them what goals they were working on. Every one of them, within my first week of being there, had come to me to say someone else was not doing something they should be. It sounded like a kindergarten, and it gave me a headache. I called a meeting to get them to talk to each other, and we talked about overall strategy. We then put it into Lotus Notes, and each team could track their progress.

It fundamentally changed the execution of the group. It seems that for 5 to 10 years they had been fighting each other, and now they were finally working together. They'd grown uncomfortably numb fighting, thinking it was OK to fight every day. That was not something I wanted to be a part of, so I built this product where we aligned people and gained clarity about who does what, how they report, what they're supposed to be doing, what is expected of them, how they can get rewarded, and what type of career you can have. What started there was the foundation for the product we've built today, which is the biggest on-demand product in the world with three million users.

Just like Jim Collins says in his book, *Built to Last*, most innovation comes from frustration. I was frustrated with all of the companies Unilever and Novartis had bought, and I felt there was no clarity of purpose, and no clarity regarding what you were expected to do.

Then I basically restarted my career, just like the restart button on my computer; I just clicked it, held it for a long time, ate some humble pie, and started all over at Stanford Business School.

SM: You were at Stanford from 1999 to 2001? LD: I graduated in 1999, and it was a pretty tough time. Were you involved in technology at the time?

SM: I did three startups between 1994 and 2000. LD: You're a veteran! We're the same, then; we've survived the same battles.

SM: Your technology background is nominal by Silicon Valley standards, it seems. LD: Absolutely. At that time I was a little more humble. I thought technology was intimidating even though I had used it in my different jobs.

For example, when I was doing that merger of all those companies, people were talking a lot about the Internet, and it was funny how they were talking about it. Take the multibillion-dollar food distribution company Sysco –

> *I'm trying to explain to the CEO of my company about Cisco, and he thinks I'm talking about Sysco. I was talking about routers, and he was hearing food distribution.*

That's what it was like in big business and why Jack Welch had an initiative called *e-business* as if it were some sort of big, fancy thing. It was just a very different world.

I knew I had to figure out what the potential really was. I had a subscription to *Wired* magazine, and I found out about the Netscape Developer Conference. I decided to attend the conference in San Jose, which was the greatest thing in the world for a guy like me who had no technology background. I found a little project called NetObjects that you could build an org chart with, and I took it back to Unilever in Holland.

The VP of HR was always such a loser – he would just sit there and whine in the board meetings. I asked him finally, "Why are you always whining?" and he said, "Because nobody wants to talk to me, and everybody is always moving people around without telling me." "What the hell is wrong with you?" I said. "It's not interesting when you show up with binders of meaningless stuff; it's already outdated the second you print it."

So I brought back the NetObjects program, built everything out myself, and went to the IT department and said, "Hey, I need a server because the instructions here say I need a server." Their immediate reply – "No! We can't give you a server because we're waiting for NT." I learned that NT was something Microsoft was releasing in two years, and of course that was not going to work. I then went out and bought my own server down at the local store and charged it to the company and built a dynamic org chart and gave it to our VP of HR. It fundamentally changed his role in the company. He could now sit there and show everybody where people were moving. The whole process gave me a feel for the power of technology.

In a sense, that's how we started SuccessFactors. Through some friends at business school, I was able to find a company that had built a really great little product over the Web, and a very scalable one.

SM: Before we go there, what filled the gap between 1999 and 2001 – before SuccessFactors? LD: I thought I had to learn what all the technology was about. Another Danish guy, who'd joined some bioinformatics guys from Stanford, had started a company two years earlier, and they felt they needed some more business leadership. That's where I came in.

The other Danish guy was the CEO, and he had come over from Affymetrix. I told him I wouldn't mind being his VP because I felt I could learn a lot, although it was a big step backwards in my career to be a VP of a little startup after I had twice been CEO of a real company. But

I didn't care about the title; I cared about learning.

I met a bunch of really great engineers, and I really loved them. They were from China, India, Wisconsin, and everybody was just working together. In my own bones I started to feel the infrastructure of Silicon Valley. I had no clue about any of that; you don't read about that anywhere! The CEO was at McKinsey, then business development at Affymetrix — he had never run a team, ever, and that was something I'd been doing for five years already. People could not talk to him; he built this little box for himself, and would sit inside his office while all the engineers came and found me to find out what they were supposed to be doing.

I learned how to manage engineers. Engineers think differently; they are so much smarter than the average bear. If you don't argue extremely succinctly and exhaustively with them and explain all the data, and you try to just tell them business speak, they don't listen to you. But if you can explain the basics, all the data from the ground up, and give them the true logical answer regarding why you are doing something, then you have them bought in, and they'll work incredibly hard for you.

SM: When working with smart people, it always pays to explain the *why*. LD: Exactly, and they'll ask 15 questions to get there if they need to. To this day I adore them. They cannot do anything until they know why. I love that. That was the biggest takeaway for me: how to manage an engineering team. I didn't know what I was going to learn; I knew I would learn something, but I didn't know it was going to be that.

But I just could not get along with this guy who was the CEO, because he couldn't see the value I brought. He would say that we just needed to get people to do stuff, and that's not how it works, at least for me. I have to get people involved and engaged. We had a big split, so I left.

I was sitting around thinking, "What should I do now? I guess I'll have to start my own company." That's what I always wanted to do, and now there were no more excuses. That was it; I started SuccessFactors.

SM: What was the genesis of SuccessFactors? How did you bring people together? You're not an engineer, so you weren't the person building the product. LD: I was lucky that a business school friend helped me. That was the whole idea of going to business school, so that worked.

At that time, in 2001, if you can remember that, I felt that most venture capitalists were just scurrying and running away from class action lawsuits, so afraid of getting caught. There were *a lot* of class action lawsuits at the time. It was like bargain hunting time. Nothing cost anything because people didn't think of ventures as a cost; they thought of them in terms of "How can we get out of this? How can I get rid of it?" There were a bunch of great technologies out there, but they didn't have any great products coming out of them.

The first thing I discovered was that these technologies were run by people who had never managed anything. It took me two minutes to realize. I would sit there with the CEO of a company I wanted to buy, and I could see straight through him. Out of respect I would ask, "What's your background?" and I would get an answer like, "I used to run customer success at Symantec." I would then think, "Oh, OK. Now you're the CEO? What the hell are you talking about? Those things have nothing to do with each other!"

It was like that everywhere I went. I would ask their venture capitalists and be told they had just run out of CEOs. That was my advantage – I knew how to manage. So I basically bought two different companies that were completely broken.

SM: Could you explain how you bought them? Where did you get the money? LD: I didn't have any money, so I got clever. I went to an auction in Redwood City, and they were selling these dotcoms every three minutes, and it was the greatest thing. If I had had more brain power and capacity, I would have stayed around and bought more stuff.

What had happened was all these credit companies had gone and taken ownership of these broken companies; they had secured rights in the company. It's called a UCC 1 filing. When you have a UCC 1, you have the keys to the castle; you own everything – IP and the whole freaking thing. They just shut these companies down, but they wanted something in return, so they'd try to sell them at these auctions.

I just went in there and made a credit bid, which means I said, "I'll take on the debt for this company personally."

> *I don't remember how old I was, maybe 31, and I was taking on $3.2 million in debt to own this company. I figured I would do whatever I could to build it up.*

SM: Quite a show of courage! How did you find this particular company that you ended up acquiring? LD: From a friend who sat next to me in business school. He was at a venture firm, so he knew all the good companies that simply didn't have leaders.

SM: Which venture firm? LD: It was Foundation Capital. He told me about the first one, and the founding father of Foundation Capital told me about the other technology firm – a big, scalable, on-demand platform, which is really the most interesting thing I bought. The other thing I bought was really worthless; it had a little bit of sales, maybe $100,000 or $200,000. But non-event.

SM: What was the name of the on-demand platform? LD: It was called eAlity. I was as lucky as it gets, but at least I was smart enough to jump on it. The guys that built that were three Chinese supercomputing geniuses who had all come from Hong Kong and met at Berkeley. They had built this twice already. Talk about pioneering On Demand – they were way before anyone else. They had a Concur-like product before Concur did. These guys had built an outstanding, one-code, scalable supercomputing platform, but they didn't have a CEO. They had that customer success guy who did nothing for them.

The interesting thing was that the other company I bought had some interesting applications, but the apps server was complete crap and could not scale. We had two Pentium 286s that would run this proprietary architecture that was such crap that when we had more than four customers, who had in combination 800 users, the computers would just stop.

SM: Why did you buy that one? LD: I thought the applications were very, very interesting. They had very clever content on how to do a writing assistant. That's the thing that still survives in the company we have today. It lets you sit down and write a review for somebody when you don't know exactly what to write.

SM: So, in this portfolio of "stuff" you bought, you had the distributed computing infrastructure, and you had a tiny bit of the SuccessFactors application. Is that correct? LD: You nailed it. I'm amazed that with all the garbage that's come out of my mouth that you get that, but that is exactly what happened.

SM: I'm in the business of synthesis. LD: You're cutting right through. I bought a bunch of shit, and two things came out: a distributed architecture and a little bit of a product.

SM: Was Foundation out of the game at this point? LD: That's the funny thing. My friend left Foundation because they didn't pull the trigger on SuccessFactors. And I just felt he should have gotten something, so before the IPO, I gifted him some shares. He e-mailed me yesterday after the earnings call and said he still thinks about that point seven years ago when they had the chance to own 40% of SuccessFactors, and he still cannot believe Foundation could not pull the trigger.

SM: The venture business is full of stories like this. LD: Oh my God, it is. It is incredible. The super geniuses and the wonder boys just ignored me while I was presenting my life's dream. I was just sitting there thinking, "Wow, these guys have gotten way too rich, way too early to completely ignore me this way."

SM: And by having done way too little. LD: Exactly – so imagine I'm standing there presenting what I've been preparing for 15 days for these big, important venture capitalists, and they're playing with their shoes.

SM: What you're bringing up is an issue many entrepreneurs have experienced: a total disrespect and arrogance on the part of the VCs. They forget that the sole basis of their existence is to *serve* entrepreneurs, not the other way around. So, who finally funded your dream? LD: David Strohm from Greylock.

SM: How did you get to David? LD: He was involved in one of the companies, and he was the most skeptical – that's why I liked him. I don't like people you can win over easily. He just sat there and looked at me like, "Who the hell are you, and what do you know about anything?"

SM: You probably didn't know anything about anything. LD: I didn't, and that's exactly what I said to him, and that's how he tells the story. He just says, "OK, I'll give you a million, and you see what you can do with it. That's it. You are never going to get anything more if you don't do something incredible with it."

SM: Then what happened? LD: We launched the product three days after 9/11. That seems to be the theme of this company. We went public when the markets were down 9% more than they had been in five years. We're used to it now.

SM: Were you able to funnel in all of the ideas of aligning arrowheads, appraisals, etc. into the product? LD: Yes. That's what I'm most proud of in my career. We have truly built a product where people can say, "We can see everybody's goals, and everybody knows what they are supposed to do."

SM: Is that the value proposition of SuccessFactors? LD: A big part of it, yes. Another aspect of it is that you get employees engaged at a level they've never been before. We've found that it drives top-line performance 2–3%. It's incredible, but it's so simple. Have you heard of the band Dire Straits?

SM: Sure. LD: He has a song, "Industrial Disease." It's like this industrial disease that you don't care about your employees anymore, and it's OK not to care about them. First of all, that's pretty inhuman not to care, but aside from that, it's a dumb business decision.

> *Why would you not focus on these assets, which are 70% of your costs? Why would you not sit down and look them straight in the eyes and say, "Are you part of the future? Are you in? Because if not, please go somewhere else. Otherwise, let's get together around this."*

It is such a basic principle, but companies have allowed themselves to stop doing it. Bad companies certainly have.

SM: You're now taking your solution to companies and helping them with this rather key alignment function that nobody else does. LD: That's right. From that, we drive 360-

degree reporting, succession planning, and a very nice interactive org chart where you can see who's at risk of leaving and who wants to be promoted. You can put in, "I want to go here, I want to go there."

You can actually manage your team. You can determine which people go on which seats on the bus – that's a new product we built three years ago which has had a lot of success. In fact, Goldman Sachs and Healtheon both started with that product before they went to the alignment products.

I'm always confused what to answer when people ask if our value proposition is only alignment. That is where the company started, but some of these other products have gotten real traction and are a real percentage of our sales.

Another one that a lot of companies start with is compensation. The compensation product was very hard to build, but it's something I had in my very first product in Lotus Notes, where if you do your goals you're probably going to ask what you're going to get out of it. I will tell you what you're going to make if you meet your goals, what you're going to make if you exceed your goals, and what you're going to make if you fail on your goals. It's really simple.

> *I'm not that money hungry, but I always told my bosses that I want to know what I'm going to get paid. You're going to be extremely clear to me about what I'm going to make.*

You would be amazed how many people do not know how much more money they can make on bonuses.

SM: The "mush" factor in corporations is amazing. LD: That is a beautiful word for it.

Now we have products through which you know what people you need in different roles. Now you need to recruit people to fit into those slots, so we built a recruiting product to get them into the right places and get them on board in the right way, where they have clear expectations when they get into the job.

Then we have products that allow us to track what happens when you fire somebody. How is it that we are losing people in engineering, and we are not losing anybody in sales – is that hurting us?

Then we have a career development tracking tool to make sure people can see that they have a career. We also have an internal directory; apparently people have never built easy-to-use directories which use a lot of fun technology where we have tag clouds – it's very much like an enterprise Facebook. We use it over the Blackberry so you can find different people, find out who they work with.

SM: It's an internal LinkedIn. LD: That's exactly what it is.

SM: Do you also have people outside the firewall of the company, like consultants and partners? LD: We do on one of the products, the 360.

Here people link with others in the network as a whole, and they can link outside of the company on that. I met the CEO of a very small company who said we had changed his company. I asked him how, and he said, "Over the last 10 years I had entrusted my company to another guy and sort of felt there was something going on but never really knew what it was. But then I got these 360 reports with outside vendors, accountants, and everybody commenting said he was an asshole. Everybody! So I found out I had hired a guy who was an asshole, and I was like holy shit – he's not an asshole with me, but he is with everybody else!"

SM: A 360 is a very powerful tool. LD: It changed my career.

SM: How do you view your competitive landscape right now? The HR, human capital landscape is moving online and becoming very big, penetrating more of the mid-market and small businesses. How do you view the rest of the players in your ecosystem, and how do you position? LD: Let's just look at the facts – I'll talk to you like an engineer because that's how I've learned to speak now. We are in 13,000 opportunities at the moment, and the competitor we've met the most, we've only encountered 17 times. Our biggest competitor is not another software vendor; it's companies doing nothing.

SM: Who was the competitor you met 17 times? LD: That happened to be Kenexa. But we have very little in common with them. They're a big recruiting firm, and they do a lot of surveys. They're a 20-year-old company – now they claim to be an on-demand company.

I can promise you, you don't change a 20-year-old company in three years, which is why they missed a quarter two quarters ago, in a big way, and their stock got completely slammed. You cannot miss a quarter like that if you have a true on-demand company, so in my mind that clearly settled that they are not an on-demand company once and for all. They're in a bunch of deals where we're replacing them, like MetLife and American Airlines.

SM: There are a lot of opportunities – companies just aren't doing anything in this space. LD: Yes! Over 80% of our deals are people who are sitting there with a spreadsheet, and we come in and talk to them and tell them to try something else because it's just so quick, so cheap, and it transforms companies.

SM: How do you view Taleo? LD: I think they had a lot of success with enterprise accounts in recruiting, then they bought RecruitForce, which was a complete copy of SalesForce.com, and now they've just started to launch something in our space because they see what we're doing.

Launching and doing are different things, though. I'll tell you what we have – we have 100 companies with 10,000 users. This is something SalesForce.com can only dream about. I have seven VPs from SalesForce.com, and they say they'd die to have 10,000-user organizations – they have two now.

The impact we've had over the last seven years, the traction we have, the depth and the brand recognition, that means it'll be really difficult for somebody to catch up.

The second part is that a lot of companies do not care about people, but we do at this company. I hired every single person up to 300 myself, and most of them are still here.

SM: How many people do you have now? LD: We have 700. The first three years of this company's life was cash flow positive. We saw what we had: a doubling of customers every year. We knew when SAP and Oracle saw this they were going to go crazy, so we knew we had to run. We embarked on a very aggressive strategy in 2004. I mean it was *very* aggressive. It was to completely dominate the market in terms of products, markets – small, medium, large – and geographies. That's something I am not confused about. I ran global products at Unilever. I was on the board of a global company. For me it is not hard to think about being global.

When we launched the product, we already had users internationally. Today we have it in 22 languages; it is being used in 156 countries. We don't just have a sales rep or a channel partner; we have our own people on the payroll doing implementations.

SM: How did you go from 2001, with $1 million in financing, to the scale you are today? Didn't you have to finance the company further? LD: I basically didn't have a life for six years.

SM: Didn't you also need more financial resources? LD: When you're cash flow positive, you don't need any more money. That's the funny thing. For the first three years, we didn't spend any more money. I got a new investor in from Texas Pacific Group in 2003, and I still remember him in every board meeting saying, "I can't believe it; you still haven't spent any of my money."

SM: Who was that? LD: That was Dave Whorton.

SM: I thought so. LD: You know him? Do you like him?

SM: Yes, he's a good guy. LD: I think he's a great guy. I'm an investor in his new fund. He had me at hello. I'd decided I wasn't going to take any more money from anybody, but he changed me. He came in and said, "Wow, this is emotional intelligence on steroids over the Web." "Now you're flirting with me," I said. "This isn't fair!" We spent six hours in a conference room discussing, and I finally said, "OK, you can invest." He was the real deal.

SM: How much money did you take from Dave? LD: I think it was $5 million.

SM: All in all, in the history of the company, what kind of investment have you required? LD: I did get comfortable raising money, unfortunately. I raised another $45 million. I got Eric Dunn in at that time. What we decided to do with Dave is that we would go for the big bucks and we would go all out.

We began investing in the mid-market. In 2003 and 2004, that seemed like a very ambitious project as it was essentially trying to do two things. Something I had learned at Unilever is if you give somebody a real responsibility, give them a budget, then you can make things like that happen. We separated out and built a business in the mid-market, and it did well.

Since it did well, I was comfortable going to Europe, but I didn't want to destroy the focus of the company, so I did it on my own and let the team do what it was doing. I went to Europe every week on my own, and I didn't even tell my board because they said Europe was too complicated. Then I closed a $2.5 million deal in December 2005 with Lloyds Bank in London, and the board changed their tune.

Then we decided to invest more boldly and took $5 million from Eric Dunn. We saw that this stuff was working, and we had enterprise and mid-market — we were doing Europe, so should we try Asia and should we try channels? We decided to do it, and we did that with Eric Dunn's money, and it worked as well.

We then saw this business was really working. Should we try to go into small business, which is the biggest market in the world? Eric Dunn knows the small business market, and he felt we could do it. Small business doesn't have the luxury of having a huge staff to help them, so the product ideas are so crisp, clean, and lovely that it was worth doing just for that.

SM: You don't face as much competition in small business, either. LD: No, you don't. There is no competition. That was Eric Dunn's decision point on the board. We brought in Emergence Capital, who focuses on On-Demand and SMB. They put in $10 million, and we really built a small business "company" inside the company. We hired the VP of sales from SalesForce.com, Shelly Davenport, to run it. That's now our fastest growing business; we have 50 reps there, and it's going really, really well.

SM: What is the revenue split between small, medium, and large businesses? LD: Out of new business, US Enterprise is 60%. The other key areas, small, medium, and Europe, are all close to 10% each. The rest is split between Asia Pacific and Channels. We'll do deals with IBM and EDS. We just did a fantastic deal with Marriott.

SM: What's the structure of the deal with Hewlett or EDS? Is it that they have BPO operations, and they use your systems to power it? LD: What happened since 2001 is that the BPOs all gave up having their own products. They had enough problems making money on their BPO structures. They literally take our stuff, put it in their brochures, and we do everything from there on out. They're pretty nice deals.

SM: You're basically outsourced BPO for them? LD: You could say that. They're 10-year deals.

SM: So they're channel deals? LD: Yes, they are. That's it. It's a pretty basic story. We're now three million users in 156 countries. We went up from one and a half million in 16 months. We announced that we are the fastest growing on-demand company in the world – 95% year on year.

SM: Talk about the highlights of your earnings that you just announced. LD: That is one highlight right there – we grew 95%. We grew faster than Omniture and SalesForce.com going into the IPO, and coming out of it we just announced this 95% growth.

The other key elements are that we felt very strongly that we have no negative indicators. All of the deals are up, our seat prices are up, our products are all selling, so we're blessed. It's been a lot of hard work for a long time. Now we're investing a lot of money. The positive is that we have $46 million in bookings in Q4, which actually only translates to $19 million in revenue – just so you can see how conservative we are. Bookings are money we collect immediately, so it's not like it's not real. It's first year value. We cannot recognize the revenue because we're very conservative on that. Unlike NetSuite, we decided not to stop doing long-term deals. They decided to stop doing long-term deals so they can recognize everything immediately.

SM: You have the advantage of backlogs. LD: Exactly! We love it. So what if Wall Street can't understand it in the short term. It doesn't matter; we're in it for the long term.

SM: Very early on in this conversation, you mentioned your devotion to metrics. Talk about metrics you track, metrics you manage your company by. LD: We can start with late-stage pipeline coverage. That's how I know our business is healthy. Late-stage pipeline coverage of each area and each sector is probably how we have been successful in all these areas.

You asked about Taleo, and I think that's because you met with their CEO, so you're close to that business now. They talked on their earnings call about how they made a massive investment in SMB, how they have 12 reps, but we started in 2003 and in small business alone we have 50. We also have a bigger mid-market business, so that tells you a little about the investment we've made; it's almost 10 times what they have. I don't decide to address those things in my earnings call, but that gives you a feel for the size and the scope we have.

How we get successful metrics is by tracking every single rep. I have all of these employees who worked at Oracle and other places, and when I asked them what their pipeline was, their answer would be, "Oh, it's big." I would then ask, "No, what is your late-stage coverage ratio on your quota?" They looked at me like a deer in headlights: "What?!" I then repeat, a bit slower, "Late-state coverage ratio on your quota?" and usually get something like, "Well, that's a lot of math!" My answer: "Let's talk again when you've done the math."

That's how I run the company.

I ask what the average price per seat was, per module? Nobody does that. They just say, "It was a big deal!" But so what? That does not matter. We need to know if we're going to make money on it, so let's break it apart.

If you work at a blue chip, top performing Fortune 10 global company, that's normal for you, but every single person I have working here, including the three best sales reps from Taleo, and we just hired the best one from Oracle, and two guys from SAP in Europe, they come over and talk about the big deals. But what I want to know is if they were profitable, or did you give the product away? They look at me and they know I'm talking about the right thing and that they're going to learn a lot because they're going to work at a very different level.

We consider ourselves some sort of mixture between the Navy Seals and McKinsey, and that's how we go to work.

> *We actually had the head of the Navy Seals come and speak to us at our last all-hands meeting, to give you a feel for how we operate and how we think of ourselves. Across the business we track metrics like that.*

We track productivity; we track things we've invented ourselves such as *ramp sales equivalents,* which talks about how much a rep should be producing right now. Not just if he's a good guy or a bad guy, but how long has he been here compared to everybody else. With this internal ramp sales metric, which we use for both professional services and customer success, we can talk about the capacity we expect from a particular person, from a region, from an aggregation of regions, from all the VPs – that is how we run the company.

SM: What does it cost to buy a SuccessFactors solution?
LD: It ranges. We have multimillion-dollar deals. We just told Wall Street – we want to ensure they know we have a good future, so we did something we normally would not do – that in the first five weeks of 2008 we did a million-dollar deal in retail because we know that sector has been hit very hard. And we did a million-dollar deal in financial services. At the same time, I saw a deal done yesterday for $5,000 for a 10-person company. It really depends on how many products you buy and how many seats you take.

SM: Monthly or yearly? LD: Per year.

SM: What has been the impact of the market slowdown? It seems like financial services and retail have both produced good deals in the middle of all this. LD: We're not a transactional company just sitting and figuring out where people work in the company; we're at the core of the company, deciding how to run the business. That's why people find we can help them drive top-line sales 2–3%, and do it cheaper. When you do both of those, even in a tight economy, people want to buy your stuff.

SM: How much backlog would you predict right now? LD: Our deferred revenue went up to about $101 million. In addition, we have the off–balance sheet backlog, clients like Yahoo! and REI. They bought a five-year deal, which means we have this non–balance sheet lock-in backlog that we don't talk to anyone about. We continue to excite investors for the long term, and we don't need to blow ourselves up. Nobody in the world is growing faster than us right now, and we have another secret that we're going to reveal later.

SM: Your growth strategy is organic? LD: 100% organic.

SM: I'm curious if there's anyone you want to acquire. LD: Unlike many in the Valley, I've had numerous experiences with mergers and acquisitions. I've asked many people, and there just aren't that many successful acquisitions done. When you have a good thing going, you can destroy it by doing acquisitions. I would never say never, but it's not on the top of my mind.

We did $112 million in bookings in six years. We talked about Kenexa, which is a 20-year-old company who just barely did $100 million, and they bought two recruiting companies that were struggling. I had the opportunity to buy both of those firms; they called me up and asked if I was interested in acquiring them. I told them, "I'll take a look at you, but I'm warning you I'm going to go very deep and look at every single one of your metrics you've never looked at yourself. I'm going to send you a spreadsheet, and I would like you to fill that out; if you fill that out, then we can talk." Just watching them fill that out tells me whether I can work with them, or if they're already choking.

> *SM: Were they willing to fill out the spreadsheet you sent over? LD: Most people are like, "This is insane — what are you, a root canal?"*

This is just how I do business.

Everyone in this company knows this. I finish every single all-hands meeting committing everyone to outstanding performance. It's an unbelievable rush; there is so much passion it feels like we're in the NFL. I ask, "Are you passionate about what we're doing? Are you committed to working harder than you ever have in your life? If not, you should get the fuck out the company because I don't want to work with you. If you're a slacker, find the government or some other startup — we're the real deal."

Getting that kind of commitment from people means you can routinely ask for data and they give it to you.

We go to other companies who are like, "Huh? What?" If they're asked about the pipeline by the board, they say, "It's up." What does that mean? It is very easy to get leads. You can send out a Web campaign and get people to respond. An offer for a free iPod will get you 10,000 leads, but it can be a local farmer, not someone that will help your business.

SM: I'm going to ask one last question, which is more a macro question about the segment and how Wall Street is just learning to understand these SaaS companies. What is your experience with that? LD: My experience is that they are doing exactly what you just said: they are learning. There are a bunch of them that get it. Look at us. In recognized revenue we are at $32 million for 2007. You can say Taleo and Kenexa don't do what we do, but if you consider them an HCM, they are both $100 million and $200 million companies respectively, and they are valued the same as we are. Somehow, even though technically they look bigger, Wall Street is recognizing some of the potential we have since we're receiving the same exact valuation of $500 million. I think if you look at Omniture, it has really been valued richly.

SM: Concur has been valued richly also. LD: I think you're right. Wall Street is trying to get it, but they're very confused. Companies like Kenexa don't really help them. When Kenexa tells them they're an on-demand company and then they miss a quarter by 20%, it's obvious they are not.

SM: I don't know if you saw my *Forbes* article, but I wrote about that. A true SaaS company should not be missing quarters. LD: I read that article; I didn't know that was you! I loved that article. I showed that to my whole company because it was nice that somebody finally freaking gets it!

SM: It has been a pleasure, Lars. LD: You too. I thought your energy was fabulous, which is why I got so engaged here today. You're a lot of fun to talk to and obviously know what you're doing.

Epilogue

In January 2009, in the midst of raging financial crisis and a deep global recession, I hosted an online entrepreneurship forum for laid-off engineers who were considering a switch to entrepreneurship. There were 220 people registered for the event, and 130 attended. About 145 questions were submitted, from which we synthesized some of the most commonly asked. Among those was one I want to close this volume with: How do you overcome the fear of failure?

When I was younger, I had an enormous fear of failure. I was quite used to winning, and I was very bad at losing. Since then, while I've been successful in many ways, I've also failed at various attempts. My attempt at building a product company out of India in 1997 succeeded somewhat, but the company did not become a revolutionary brand of the order that I aspired for, nor did it achieve any significant scale. Somewhere along the way, though, I developed the wisdom to take things in stride, embrace failure, learn from it, and rise above it.

When I look back on my journey to trace the development of that wisdom, I see one overriding theme. Very early in life, I developed a personal philosophy. An unlikely juxtaposition of ideas culled from various systems of thought – from the Upanishads and Vedanta, from Hindu scriptures, Ayn Rand's *Atlas Shrugged* and *The Fountainhead*, and certain Buddhist ideas of Nothingness.

The Hindu system of thought has a very powerful core concept: *Tat Tvam Asi*. I Am He. Instead of worshipping an external God, the Hindus believe that God is inside. A powerful way of thinking, since if the ultimate perfection lies inside you, and all you need to do is realize your own potential, then much of your fundamental self-doubt vanishes. At least at an existential level, the individual is complete *within*.

Ayn Rand offers a similarly individualistic perspective, although from a radically different point of view. Rand's heroes and heroines move mountains. Although reared in a communist and collectivist Russian background, Rand celebrates individual achievement and believes in one man's ability to make a difference. Many entrepreneurs I know have been influenced by Rand's writings and have drawn inspiration especially from the character of Hank Rearden in *Atlas Shrugged*, who fights on against all odds with tremendous resilience. Similar self-confidence echoes in *The Fountainhead's* architect hero, Howard Roark, whose resilience and personal integrity propel him toward a vision of architecture condemned by his contemporaries for its bold originality and threatening innovation.

Yes, conviction and faith are incredibly important components of a sustainable personal philosophy, but where does it come from? How do you develop it?

This is a question you must ask yourself. I can offer pointers on what to study, but how your own psyche will respond to the stimulus — I cannot tell. This is a spiritual, experiential journey, and you have to go it alone.

I will, however, share three more components from my own bag of wisdom: laughter, compassion, and Nothingness. When the individualistic ideology overwhelms, when your head swells with self-aggrandizement, think of yourself in respect to the Himalayas. Or the Pacific Ocean. Or the universe.

We are nothing. We are insignificant. We are a single speck of dust in the continuum of time.

So why be afraid of failure?

Made in the USA